SPIRITUAL MINDSET

SPIRITUAL MINDSET

Daniel T. Mangrum

SPIRITUAL MINDSET
Copyright 2020 Daniel T. Mangrum
Published by AGD Publishing Company

All rights reserved.

No part of this book may be reproduced, distributed or transmitted in any form by any means, graphic, electronic, or mechanical, including photocopying, recording, taping, or by an information storage or retrieval system, without permission in writing from the publisher, except in the case of reprints in the content of reviews, quotes or references.

Printed in the United States of America
Second Edition: 978-1-7346758-2-5
First Edition: 978-1-7346758-0-1

Special discounts are available on bulk quantity purchase by book clubs, associations and special interest groups. For details email: allisongdaniels@verizon.net or call (202) 258-4987. For information log on to: www.agdpublishing.com

CONTENTS

Acknowledgements   v
Dedication   vi

Chapter 1   1
Faith! What Is It?

Chapter 2   9
Faith Exercises Your Mind

Chapter 3   15
How Do You Think?

Chapter 4   25
Your Mental Capacity

Chapter 5   31
My Thinking – An Asset or Liability?

Chapter 6   37
To Think

Chapter 7   49
It's All About the Way You Think

Chapter 8   55
The Interchange Between Spirit, Soul and Body

Chapter 9   61
Processing Problems

Chapter 10   67
The Power of Remembering

ACKNOWLEDGEMENTS

There are many wonderful people who contributed, directly and indirectly in many countless ways to my experiences in writing this book – to you I say thank you.

My sincere gratitude to my family, who generously shared me with this manuscript. I will always appreciate your love and support. I also want to acknowledge the compassion and encouragement that I consistently received from my church family. May this book encourage and bless you all.

Thank you to everyone working with AGD Publishing Company, who helped me get this second book project to print and distributed. I pray that it blesses you mightily.

Most of all, I acknowledge with a grateful heart to God who is the head of my life, who inspired and made this project possible.

DEDICATION

I wish to dedicate this book to my loving parents who were such great examples and an inspiration of genuine Christianity, who displayed and taught me the love of Jesus. To my Mother who was my first Bible teacher and my Dad who is the man I admire most in this world; to you both, I love you and I appreciate you –many thanks.

For over 30 years I have been blessed to be married to the most beautiful and amazing woman on this earth, Sabrina Mangrum. Sabrina, I express to you my sincere gratitude for being such a devoted soul mate and help mate; dear, I love you.

I am so grateful to be the father of three beautiful, talented and wonderful children, April, Danielle and Diamond. You are so much more than my children to me – each of you is my dearest friend. I love you.

I want to thank the members of Cornerstone Peaceful Bible Baptist Church for allowing me to serve as your Pastor for all these years. Truly, it has been a rewarding and delightful experience, as we all walk this Christian journey together. I thank God every day for you. Love you all.

Above all, I thank the Lord Jesus Christ, our soon Coming Conquering King, for being my Savior, my Lord and my Best Friend.

I love you all.

CHAPTER 1

FAITH! WHAT IS IT?

When I first started writing this book, I thought it would be about faith but half-way through, I realized this is not just about faith. This is about how to live. Since the Bible says "the just shall live by faith" I now understand that faith is a means to an end. Faith helps you to live. The point of faith is not faith alone, by itself, but how it helps you to know how to live. Faith enables you to know how you can relate to God. It gives you a way to navigate through the challenges of life. Faith is what we draw upon in order to live. Without faith it is not possible to live fully. That is because you cannot relate to God without having faith. The only way to truly live is to be connected to God by faith. And so, while our aim is to discuss faith in this book, it is in the context of helping or empowering us to know how to live a better quality of life.

We need faith to handle the situations we face every day. We need faith to maintain quality relationships in marriage, parenting and family in general. As finite beings we are constantly coming into situations where our human resources are not enough. The nature of life is that so much is out of our control. We have no idea what is going to happen next. So many things can go wrong at any time.

It is our faith that is our only comfort. Faith is the only thing we can find security in. It is our faith in God that is literally our only hope. We are kidding ourselves if we think we are in control. We are delusional if we think we can dictate anything on our own. We are all dependent and reliant on a God who is our chief provider and protector. Faith is not an option. Faith is the only option. To not believe in God is to ignore the reality that we are merely human beings. Faith is the only way we are to live.

God is accessed by our faith in Him. We cannot please Him without faith. The basis of our relationship with God is by faith. Our connection to God is through faith. The transmission of God's power is through faith. And so, nothing can be more important than understanding about faith.

Understanding how faith works is the most important survival tool any one of us can have. Utilizing faith is the only way we can make it. It is by faith that we have what we need to overcome the challenges of life. Life without faith is scary and unstable. If your hopes are in yourself, you are clearly in over your head. As Paul says in 1 Corinthians, "If in this life alone we have hope we are above all people most miserable." *1 Corinthians 15:19*

For example, if you do not have faith in God, how do you handle the subject of death? How do you get past the death of a loved one? Without faith how do you recover from major disappointments? Is it not faith in God that allows you to face a difficult and uncertain future? Without faith, not only will you die hopeless, but you will live an unfulfilled and purposeless life.

Jesus came to reveal God to us. His mission was to connect us to God. He showed us who God was and what God requires of us. If you take faith out of the equation Christianity is an empty religion. Faith is the essence of what it means to be a Christian. Using faith is how we are to function as children of God.

I realize faith is a subject that has been dealt with by so many other Christian authors. I dare say it is one of the most talked about subjects in Christian circles, although still, some of the greatest Christian thinkers have never fully covered this important subject. I believe, however, that God has given me some insights of which I can add to the discussion. I am not suggesting that what I offer in this book is something that no one has ever thought of before; I can only expound on the insights I want to offer that have been life changing for me. After over 40 years of being a student of the Word, somehow the things I recently learned had a profound effect on my life. In this book

I want to share what I have learned about faith; my hope is that you too will experience a change for the better.

First, to believe, is to think something is true. Given this definition, thinking is an integral part of what it means to believe. So, we begin with the assumption that thinking is the foundation of believing. Put another way, it is your thinking that is the basis of your faith. Faith is a mindset. That means you literally believe out of the mindset you have. When your thinking is flawed, you have difficulty believing. This is because your mindset is either weak or not yet established. Faith is that mindset that must be fed by sound thinking based on truth, the Word of God. When that mindset is in place, believing is possible.

I came to conclude from my study that these two words –thinking and believing –are so closely aligned that you could say that in a lot of ways thinking and believing are synonymous. Every place where you see believe in the Bible you can say or put think in its place, and it means the same thing. For example, see *Matthew 8:13*, "And Jesus said unto the centurion, Go thy way; and as thou hast believed, so be it done unto thee. And his servant was healed in the selfsame hour." When Jesus was ministering to the Centurion who had come to Him asking Him to heal his servant, Jesus closes that account out by saying to him "Go thy way, and as thou as believed, so be it done unto you. And his servant was healed in the selfsame hour." Actually, you could substitute the word think with the word believe and it could mean, Go thy way, and as thou have thought (think), so be it done unto you.

Another example is in *Matthew 9:28*, "And when he was come into the house, the blind men came to him: and Jesus saith unto them, Believe ye that I am able to do this? They said unto him, Yea, Lord." Immediately following the miracle of raising Jairus' daughter, these two blind men literally followed Jesus into a house crying, "thou son of David have mercy on us." When they cornered Jesus in the house, Jesus says to them, "believe ye that I am able to do this?" Once again you could replace believe with think and get the same meaning. "Do you think I can do this?" Jesus tells them too, "According to your faith be it unto you."

According to your thinking be it unto you, might mean the same thing. Now, back to Jairus. When Jesus told him to believe only, I ask you, wasn't He saying think only on what I told you and ignore what the messenger from your house just said? When you look at it this way, you realize that believing is a mental function. It is the result of you applying your mental faculties. You are determining from your thoughts what you are accepting as true. When Thomas said in *John 20:25*, "... Except I shall see in his hands the print of the nails, and put my finger into the print of the nails, and thrust my hand into his side, I will not believe." Wasn't he then saying that he (Thomas) would not think what they told him to be true?

This has been a game changer for me because all these scriptures where Jesus is teaching about faith really are about Jesus teaching about thinking. When Jesus is teaching us to believe, He is talking about changing how we think. In times past when I had taught about how Jesus was building up the faith of the disciples, I now understand that Jesus was really trying to raise their level of thinking. It was more about getting them to expand their thinking.

As a matter of fact, in my opinion, you are wasting your time trying to get people to believe when you have not addressed their flawed way of thinking.

It is better to focus on the thinking than it is to focus on the believing. Believing is not possible if your thinking is not up to what you are believing. In reality, thinking drives your believing instead of your belief driving your thinking. You cannot get yourself to think correctly by believing, but you can get yourself to believe by appropriate thinking.

The natural flow is to think to believe, however, you can't believe to think.

Thinking allows you to understand. Understanding is critical to believing. You cannot believe fully anything that you don't understand. It is not a situation where you can just leave your mind out and believe anyway. I realize we cannot understand everything we believe, but understanding, no doubt, strengthens our capacity to believe. Arguably, I would say that there must be some understanding of what is true to really believe something.

Believing is thinking (or thoughts) to be true. Based on this simple definition, I would suggest that a few other important considerations can be made. With this being the case, this means the Word of God finds entrance into your spirit through your mind. When the mind is shut down or closed, the Spirit cannot receive the Word. The mind is not separated from the recreated human spirit. The Spirit and the mind are so intertwined that whenever you think of something, it automatically affects your spirit. Anything that is in your spirit affects how you think. Consequently, great faith is the result of great thinking. The idea that you can be spiritual and at the same time you don't involve your mind, cannot be true. Your spirituality depends on the exercise of your mind. Intelligence is critical to our spiritual condition as believers.

Consequently, the emphasis must be on the development of the mind. My faith is built by enhancing my thinking. The key to having great faith is having a sharp mind. Meditation on the Word of God is so critical. Quality time thinking on and about the Word of God allows for the Word of God to become internalized. The parable of the sower and the seed is about the process the Word of God goes through to produce results. Just as the seed must germinate, the Word of God goes through a similar process of development in our thinking. Much like the seed bears fruit, the Word bears blessings. You could argue that the soil is the mind where the Word must find favorable conditions to allow the seed to develop.

Isaiah mentions the process of the Word being like the hydraulic cycle when the rain falls and takes on the form of water vapor and returns to the sky. In a process of transformation, the Word also brings about a specific result. Another example would be how Peter mentions in his epistle that we should desire the sincere milk of the Word that we may grow thereby. In this case, just as the body takes food and converts it into heat energy for our bodies to be fueled, the Word fuels our spiritual growth.

This is also important when it comes to dealing with life's

challenges and trials. To believe is to think positive; believe and receive the Word, which is truth (to be true), especially when facing a crisis. In those situations, thinking of God's Word is the proper response. Any attention to anything other than the Word is not only counter-productive but a distraction. Focusing on the Word releases divine energy which in turn releases faith power. It is very important that you are mindful of what you put your mind on in a crisis.

Paul told Timothy in 2 Timothy 2:15 "Study to shew thyself approved unto God, a workman that needeth not to be ashamed, rightly dividing the word of truth." When you study the Word, you are equipped for the test. You increase your likelihood of performing well when you have studied beforehand. When you come up on a trial the most important thing to remember is how much Word is in you and how important it is to act on the Word that's already down on the inside of you. Do you strongly believe God's Word in the situation? You cannot just turn it off and on. It must be something you practice. Paul tells Timothy that there is the potential that if you don't study you will be ashamed of your performance.

Thinking is a skill vital in faith. Consequently, concentration is necessary for faith. Your ability to maintain and retain the Word of God without becoming distracted is the key to believing. The only way the Word of God can help you is if it is the object of your thinking. When God's Word is your central focus the effect of the Word becomes apparent.

In my opinion, there is a thinking crisis in our world. We have had so many scientific discoveries and advances in technology that our lives are drastically different from the life our ancestors lived. I believe one effect of all this is that we do less thinking than ever. I would suggest that there is a downside to all the changes. The problem is that we are so dependent on these devices and gadgets that our minds are not active enough. Anything you do not use over time will start to diminish in its effectiveness. Unfortunately, our minds are not being utilized like they were used in the past. Remembering can sometimes become a challenge, especially as we grow older, and therein we can become less effective in not remembering. Most of us do not know basic information by memory. While it may seem innocent to utilize scientific discoveries and new technology to assist us in our thinking and remembering, the danger is that we are not using our minds. Over time we lose our thinking capacity, especially our spiritual edge. Our spiritual edge can be lost because of its relationship to our belief and our faith. We have Christians who have lost their ability to think. Many do not know the scriptures by memory. They spend very little time meditating, memorizing or remembering God's Word. It is no wonder they have little faith because they have so little of God's Word stored in their minds.

You may ask, "How can this process take place where the Word becomes internalized if there is no effort to retain the Word?" The Holy Spirit can and will bring all things to your remembrance but what if you never take time to deposit the Word into your memory bank? What can the Holy Spirit bring to your remembrance if you never take time to study the Word to even remember anything?

It is sad that each year our attention span is becoming less and less. Getting people to even stay attentive for any time period is becoming almost impossible. All of this is a part of a demonic conspiracy to make us less compatible with a quality relationship with God. Things like prayer, meditation and seeking God requires quality time with Him. I strongly encourage you to study the Word and exercise your mind constantly on truth, the Word of God. An active mind is the basis for active faith. When you understand the role, your mind plays in spiritual activity, you understand why the reduction of thinking is such a threat. God's Word must become priority to be processed.

God's Word is Spirit and it is life. The Word must be active in your life, affecting and impacting you from the inside out. When the Word is internalized inside you, the Word is connecting you to God. It is literally strengthening your faith. It is empowering your mind to function at a high level. The Word is literally fuel for the mind. Much like food fuels the body, the Word fuels your spiritual actions.

The lack of faith is related to a lack of being in or studying God's Word. When you don't have the Word inside you, you don't have faith inside you. The Holy Spirit is the agent of transformation. The Holy Spirit works through the dispensing of the Word. The truth makes you free. Strongholds are lifted by replacing the lies with the truth of God's Word. The enemy is engaged in a major misinformation campaign. He wants to influence your thinking as a way of attacking your faith.

When you understand the importance of believing God's Word and the importance of remembering God's Word to be a priority, you can approach your pursuit of God through the exercise of your mind so, in the next chapter I want to talk further on the subject of exercising the mind.

CHAPTER 2

FAITH EXERCISES YOUR MIND

Jesus equated faith with people displaying creativity, resourcefulness and mental strength. For example, Jesus commended the woman with the issue of blood for her faith. When she thought, If I could but touch the helm of his garment, I know I would be healed. Jesus was impressed by her faith. He commended the Syrophoenician woman for thinking of a way she could get deliverance for her daughter when she said, "but don't the dogs eat the crumbs from under the table?" Or, what about the men who, when Jesus saw their faith when they sought ways to get the man into the house so that Jesus could heal him of palsy? What faith did Jesus see other than their resourcefulness in going through the roof? And another case is when Jesus commended the Centurion for having the foresight to not need Jesus to come to his house but merely speak the Word and his servant would be healed. Jesus announced, "I have not found such great faith, no, not in Israel."

Jesus was displeased with the disciples because earlier, when they were in the midst of the sea during a raging storm they panicked; Jesus had told them to go over to the other side; either they forgot or they did not consider the miracles of the fish and the loaves earlier. Jesus equated their faith with the ability to keep their composure. He asked His disciples "where is your faith?" (See, *Mark 6:38-55*) Clearly, the definition of faith is related to mental capacity. And remember Peter doubting that he could walk on water, (see *Matthew 14:31*) Jesus said, "O thou of little faith, wherefore didst thou doubt?" Why did Peter think differently? Faith was clearly associated with the thoughts of what he, Peter, was thinking to be true.

In Matthew 25 and Luke 19, the parables of the pounds and talent were referring to how the servants used wisdom and their shrewdness in how they handled their master's money. Once again, faith is associated with being smart and wise.

Jesus rebuked the disciples after the resurrection for them being slow to believe because they did not figure out that this was all fulfillment of scriptures. Faith is associated with processing everything in a way wherein you know and understand what had happened. All of this points to the fact that when we are talking about faith we are talking about the application of the mind.

Again, there is a direct relationship between believing and thinking. This makes believing more of a mental exercise than something that just comes over you. For example, imagination is a way you believe. Considering is a way you believe also. The way I believe is to exercise my mental faculties based on the spiritual reality of God's Word.

Further proof of this is that believing is a mental function as seen in how Jesus ministered to people. Many times, when Jesus ministered to people, He would have them to exercise their mental faculties in a way to connect them to the power of God's Word. For example, He would have them to change what they were assuming about a situation. Like the man by the pool who assumed he could not be healed. Jesus changed what he was thinking so that he could be healed. He asked him, "wilt thou be made whole?" This question challenged the underlying assumption he had made about his situation that he could not ever get healed. Changing that assumption set him up to think in terms of being healed.

Another example is when Jesus told the man with the withered hand to stretch forth his hand. The only way he could stretch forth his hand is if he changed how he thought about himself. His healing came right after he believed he was healed and could indeed stretch forth his hand. The ten lepers in the gospels are still another example. Jesus told the lepers to go show themselves to the priest. When they did that, as they went, they were cleansed. Jesus, once again, required them to think differently in order to receive what He would do for them. You do not show yourself to the priest until after you were healed. Jesus had to assume that when they went to the priest, He would declare them healed.

It changes things when you understand believing is making decisions to do something that seemed impossible to you. As I have shared previously, the command to stretch forth your hand or go show yourself to the priest are just a few examples of this. What about when Jesus said to the blind man "...Go wash in the pool of Siloam". He told the man by the pool "...Rise, take up thy bed, and walk."

To believe is to decide what you will think. Nothing shall be impossible for you means you can decide what is possible –for anything. In *Mark 11:23*, He states " ... That whosoever shall say unto this mountain, Be thou removed, and be thou cast into the sea; and shall not doubt in his heart, but shall believe that those things which he saith shall come to pass; he shall have whatsoever he saith." You are making the choice as to what you will have by a mental exercise of choosing. When you think something is true you choose to believe something is true. When you make a specific determination about someone, your belief about that person is set. The children of Israel could not believe they could drive out the Canaanites, so, because they thought they were inferior to the Canaanites and that they were as grasshoppers in their sight, then so they were grasshoppers in their own sight — just as they believed. There are things you think about yourself that make it impossible for you to believe you could ever get better in certain areas. There are things you think are true that are not true. But because you think they are true it has a profound effect on your ability in certain related areas.

Based on our earlier definition of what it means to believe, that is to think something to be true, another definition for faith is that it is a mindset. When Jesus talked about faith, He meant it in the context of a way of thinking. Faith has more to do with how you think than anything else. Your mindset is not limited to just the idea of thinking big or thinking in great ways. It also involves many other ways of thinking that can be a mindset of power and effectiveness. Herein is a list of ways of which I think can reflect mindsets: positive thinking, offensive thinking, clear thinking, thinking freely, optimistic thinking, power thinking, confident thinking, smooth thinking, peaceful thinking, focus thinking, intense thinking, conscious thinking, creative thinking, thinking without regrets, thinking without distractions, thinking without guilt, thinking without pain, thinking without doubt, thinking without limitations, thinking without fear, just to name a few.

Your mindset determines how you go about things and how you do things. For example, some things must be aggressively done while other things require some other kind of mindset. It is not just what you do but how you go about doing it that is very important. If you have a limited mindset, you can only go but so far because your mindset blocks how far you can go. When you have a victim mindset you anticipate being victimized; consequently, it is a self-fulfilling prophecy. When you have a defeated mindset, you are always assuming you will lose. A negative mindset is one processing everything negatively, through a pair of negative optic lens.

Your mindset is evident in your body language, your approach, your perspective and even your level of confidence. It is the most obvious aspect of your being. You won't succeed with the wrong mindset. It is not acceptable to have the wrong mindset. I used to think it was an individual thing or a personality issue, but now I realize the mindset must be appropriated. Everyone must adopt the appropriate mindset. God does not allow you to have just any kind of mindset. You must have a mindset conducive for Him to work through you. God's call is always a call to the proper mindset.

Whenever God called people to do something, He challenged them to have the proper mindset. You don't have a choice about what your mindset must be. You must adopt the mindset the Lord sets for you. This idea that people are different — that someone's personality means they must be a specific way, is false.

You must conform to the mindset God sets for you. For example, you cannot fight a war with a timid mindset. God told Gideon to send those people back who did not have the right mindset. Joshua was told to be strong and very courageous. Timothy was told to adopt the mindset of a soldier.

Your mindset determines if you are one who is blessed or if you are a person who is cursed. Whether you inspire people or discourage them is determined by your mindset. I ask you, are you someone who is confident or are you someone who is doubtful?

Great faith is when you can control your mental faculties and dictate to yourself what is the appropriate response, given a specific situation. You are not affected by your circumstances. You assign the right mindset and mental attitude to the situation. For example, in the Book of James, scripture says count it all joy when you fall into various trials and temptations. This is an act of your mental faculties to exert your will concerning your situation. This is an exercise of your faith. When you choose to love your enemies, you have clearly determined in your mind to do what does not come natural for you. Anyone who can love their enemies is going against what they naturally would be inclined to do if they are threatened. The whole idea of doing good to those who despitefully use you is to exercise your mental will. Being led and guided by the Spirit is to be in control of your mental faculties in such a way where you are in obedience to the Holy Spirit and not your lower nature or flesh.

Another definition related to this whole idea of faith involving the mind, for instance, is when you find the spirit of something in the Bible. The spirit of something is the mindset of something that a person has. For example, a spirit of infirmity is a mindset of weakness. A spirit of fear is a mindset of fear. We must redefine demonic oppression from the perspective of addressing particularly a mindset that has seized control of someone. This is opposed to thinking; it is something foreign that has just taken possession of the person. The demon in the gospels who called himself legion was clothed and in his right mind after he was delivered. That tells you that demonic possession is the loss of your mental faculties to a foreign power. His deliverance came as Jesus asked him what his name was. The man's rediscovery of who he was had allowed him to think in a way where he could be delivered.

It is obvious that Jesus ministered to the minds of people in order to address their affliction — bondage or disease. The mindset of the specific person He addressed was the main target of His ministry. While He clearly had power to heal diseases, cast out demons and raise the dead, there is a clear pattern in all His miracles where He addressed what was lacking in the thinking of the recipients of His ministry. This is because of several reasons. Many times, the origin of the specific recipient's problem could be traced to some problem with their thinking. The person's way of thinking had to reflect a change; they had to be open to receive from Jesus in order to receive their healing. A change in their thinking was crucial to them being able to overcome the effect of the affliction.

A change in their thinking was the key to have their deliverance becoming permanent. There were several encounters noted in the Bible where a two-part deliverance needed to take place wherein Jesus had to minister to some existing condition in the individual's mind; this gave way to a physical manifested deliverance. For example, the woman who was bent over and could in no wise lift herself up was first loosed, before she could be made able to stand up straight. The man with palsy was forgiven before he was given the ability to walk. Since Jesus ministered to the minds of people to extract healing in their bodies, how we think is critical to our overall health and wellbeing. In the next chapter I want to talk about why the way you think and how you think are so important.

CHAPTER 3

HOW DO YOU THINK?

The most impactful part of you is how you think. How you think has the greatest impact on your capabilities.

You could argue that the reason why the entire generation of Israelites died in the wilderness was because they could not change the way they thought. It was a change in thinking that Jesus worked on the most with the disciples during His earthly ministry.

Changing how you think equips you to relate to God. When you think like God you can understand Him and trust Him. When you are thinking clearly you are best able to believe. Failure to believe is the failure to think. When you think like God you can believe anything God says to you. It's as if what God says makes sense when your thinking is compatible with His thinking.

Strongholds are a problem because they affect how you think. You are in bondage when your mind thinks in a restrictive way. Double mindedness causes your mind to be engaged between two positions. There is this going back and forth, which causes the rest of you to be out of sorts. There is an instability created by the uncertainty in your mind. It is like you can't get it together. You are constantly in flux without ever gaining any sense of order and effectiveness. That is why James says you are like the reed going back and forth with the wind. This demonstrates how important the way you think is to your overall health and quality of life.

Strongholds have more to do with flawed thinking and unproductive, ineffective mental tendencies. Strongholds limit and restrict your thinking. Something that obstructs or hinders the free flow of your thoughts is a stronghold. Thoughts based on God's Word generate energy; when strongholds are present, they limit the flow of that positive energy. Consequently, they cause you to be bound and limited. When God's Word is received, believed and applied to your thinking, it replaces the false assumptions. Negative thinking is replaced with liberating truth. It is just that simple.

The energy released from your thoughts impacts upon you and others. This energy or power is the Holy Spirit at work in you. The power of the Holy Spirit is without limitation. Its range is everywhere and over anything. This power can be applied to anybody, any situation and in all circumstances. This power is unstoppable, undeniable and it is irresistible. It is more potent than anything in this world and can change anything or anyone for the better.

As a pastor I have discovered that the greatest impact I can have on people is to help them think better. You are not helping people if you are not positively affecting the way they think; you cannot help those who refuse to change their thinking. The problem Jesus had with the religious leaders is that they were not open to change their thinking. Jesus said those that are whole need not a physician. Mostly, people who already think they know everything are not teachable; they are people you cannot help. You are literally casting your pearls before swine when you are trying to convince someone who is already convinced that they know it all. Jesus said in *Matthew 11:25* that the Lord has hidden these things from the wise and prudent and revealed them to babes. The worst lie that you can ever believe from the devil is that you have arrived. It is a dangerous lie when you think you already know as much as you need to know. When you begin to think that you have got it altogether, that is when you are most vulnerable. Anytime Paul, with all of his knowledge and faith, said, in *Philippians 3* "I count not myself to have apprehended: but this one thing I do, forgetting those things which are behind, and reaching forth unto those things which are before, I press toward the mark for the prize of the high calling of God in Christ Jesus."

The Lord knows that none of us can say, honestly, that we have it altogether and that there is nothing more we need to know.

The moment your mind shuts down, your spiritual growth and maturity in Christ stops in its tracks. Whenever you start to assume you know enough, the stream of God's revelation dries up. The activity of your mind is your only hope for a spiritual mature life, which is why your mind is the battleground and target for the devil's attacks. If he can disrupt and divert your thinking, he knows he can neutralize you and render you powerless.

This power originates in your thinking. When your thinking is blocked the power cannot flow at all, which is why your mentality is so important. Mentality produces a state of being. Mindset precedes your condition. The way you think is a prelude to what you will eventually become. You do not have to speculate how you got to where you are because it started with your thinking. The beginning point, to any change for the better, is to think differently. There could be a lot of things wrong with you but still, you can make it; however, the one thing that you cannot afford to have wrong with you is having flawed thinking patterns.

When your thinking is off, you are off. Your thinking positions you to receive. It aligns you with God and makes you well suited to being blessed. When your mind is positive –when your mind is faith based –you are open to God's Word. When you think good thoughts, you release power and energy within yourself and you give off good vibes to others. You literally affect yourself and your environment by the kind of thoughts you dwell on or think about.

This is so important because your mind is the straw that stirs the drink. It is the engine that powers your entire life. What is going on in your mind has everything to do with what you can do and where you can go. It is not about what is going on outside. Relatively speaking, it is not so much about one's external circumstances, but it is all about what is the nature and content of one's thinking. You are as powerful as your thinking is appropriate. You are as effective as your thinking is productive.

Whatever you think is true about you and your circumstances, dictates what you are capable of doing. As much potential as you may have, you are limited by what your mind assigns you to be capable of doing. Since God is without limits and we have God in our lives, the question becomes what is the limitation in us? I want to suggest the limit is what you think you can or cannot do. We tend to assume God is limiting us from things we want to do but I would say we are limited more by our own estimation of what we can do. I believe that was the reasoning in Paul's saying in *Ephesians 3:20*, "Now unto him that is able to do exceeding abundantly above all that we ask or think, according to the power that worketh in us." Paul is saying, stop limiting yourself by what you ask or think because God can do so much more. He can do more than what you think you can do. For example, you can be as prosperous as you can think you can be. You can be as healthy as you think you can be. You can be as effective as you think you can be.

The children of Israel were supposed to drive the Canaanites out of the land but because they did not think they were capable in doing so, an entire generation died in the wilderness. Jesus asked the man by the pool "Wilt thou be made whole?" Jesus asked this because if he did not think he could be whole again, then nothing Jesus said to him could change his condition. The greatest limitation in you is what you think you can do. All areas of your life are dictated to by what you are thinking. You are as secure as you think you are. You are as satisfied and content as your thinking dictates. It does not matter what you may or may not have materially; it is what you think that determines whether you are poor or rich. Wealth is a mindset as well as poverty is a mindset. You are as healthy as your thinking dictates. I believe all diseases and illnesses originate from some mental malfunction. There is a direct link between your physical body and your mental condition.

I believe the reason why Jesus was such a prolific healer was because He understood this link and knew how to activate the minds of people in a way where they could reverse the effects of poor, damaging thinking. In almost every case, when Jesus ministered healing, there was some ministry to the mind first before there was a manifestation in their physical bodies. There are things that you might not think are connected to healing which have everything to do with how a person's thinking can be changed to make them open to being physically healed. For example, love is a powerful force in changing someone's mind and making them a recipient of God's healing power. I love how Jesus ministered to the woman with the issue of blood, He ministered to her sense of rejection and inner turmoil by focusing on her for having faith. He told her to go in peace which spoke to her sense of utter desperation and inner conflict.

When the disciples were panic stricken on the boat in the storm, Jesus told them "Be of good cheer; it is I; be not afraid." Once again, He is ministering to their sense of dread and fear by putting them at ease about their situation. Before the storm was calmed, He told them to gather their thoughts and get a grip on themselves. Choose to be of good cheer.

It was acceptance which healed the paralyzed man with palsy in *Mark 2:7-16*. Jesus told the man "Thy sins be forgiven thee; or to say, Arise, and take up thy bed, and walk?" Suddenly the man was able to walk. When his mind processed that he was accepted, his body was empowered to be healed. Remember the leper, who approached Jesus and stooped down and worshipped Him, saying, "Lord, if thou wilt, thou canst make me clean." Jesus said, "I will; be thou clean." Matthew 8:2 And immediately his leprosy was cleansed.

Wasn't that a change in his thinking caused by Jesus? Jesus agreeing with him was enough to give him a change in his thinking.

Jesus' ministry was about challenging people to change their thinking. Most of what He did was about getting people to think differently. When you look closely at what He said and what He did, almost every account in the gospels is about getting people to think in a way where they could relate to God. This was the way they could get their healing and deliverance. This was especially so for people who had conditions for a long period of time. For example, in the case of the man by the pool or the woman who was bent over; they had to change their thinking. What about the man whose son had been vexed with a demon since he was a child? In each case, Jesus challenged them to change their thinking. You remember the man who was feeling hopeless and frustrated because the disciples could not cast out the demon in his son, well Jesus addressed his mindset when he told him if you can believe, all things are possible.

When you think about how Jesus ministered to the disciples and prepared them for the work of God, once again He was constantly dealing with their mindset. When they said, "Let's go and die with him." Jesus dealt with that fatalistic mindset by raising up Lazarus. He even says I was glad I was not there so that you could believe. When they carried on in the storm, Jesus addressed their fearful mindset when He asked them why are you so fearful? When the disciples came upon the man who was born blind, Jesus dealt with their mindset when they asked, "Master, who did sin, this man, or his parents, that he was born blind?" That mindset of being powerless and unable to do anything about certain people was a problem. "Jesus answered, Neither hath this man sinned, nor his parents: but that the works of God should be made manifest in him" so that God's glory might be revealed. The whole thing about the feeding of the 5,000 was to address their mindset. After it was discovered that they were ready to concede that nothing could be done and that the people were going to faint on their way home, Jesus wanted to address this mindset. He was addressing their mindset when He washed their feet. He told them they had to have a servanthood mindset.

Spiritual bondage is the same as mental bondage. Spirits can take on the personality of a very particular mindset. For example, when you are possessed or oppressed by a demonic spirit, this will be some type of mindset. For example, it could be a spirit of fear, or a spirit of timidity. It could be a spirit of lying which is a mindset of lying. A spirit of heaviness is a mindset of depression or sadness. Instead of saying unclean spirit you could say an unclean mindset. That would mean a mindset dominated by impure or inappropriate thinking.

A mindset can be good or bad. For example, The Beatitudes in the Book of Matthew were about adopting the proper mindset. When Jesus says be poor in spirit He was talking about a mindset of humility and teachable. Blessed are the merciful for they shall receive mercy or Blessed are the those that mourn for they shall be comforted. Clearly, these are mindsets that they were to adopt.

When Jesus told the Samaritan woman, "Yet a time is coming and has now come when the true worshipers will worship the Father in the Spirit and in truth, for they are the kind of worshipers the Father seeks." *John 4:23* (NIV) you could note or say that mindset and truth mean the same thing. See in Romans 6, when Paul encourages us to "walk in newness of life." See, when Jesus told Thomas to not be faithless, but believe, He was talking about having a mindset of faith. In *Luke 12:29* when Jesus was gathered with an innumerable multitude of people, He said, "And seek not ye what ye shall eat, or what ye shall drink, neither be ye of doubtful mind." A doubtful mind is a doubtful mindset.

Never is this more apparent than the account of the man with the palsy in Matthew's Gospel. I have read this passage for many years, but only recently have I come to understand that this confrontation with the religious establishment was about Jesus emphasizing about the proper mindset of all believers. Matthew's account ignores the point Luke makes in his account about how the men went to the extreme measure to go up on the roof to lower the sick man on his mat through the tiles, into the middle of the crowd to place him before Jesus. In Mark's Gospel, he was more intent to get to the main point about how this was more about what happened after the man was in front of Jesus. As soon as the man comes face to face with Jesus, Jesus makes a very provocative statement. Jesus announces to him, "Son, thy sins be forgiven thee." In other words, you are no longer guilty of your sins. Basically, as of right then, Jesus was saying that He is removing any blame for anything the man had done wrong. In other words, nothing you have ever done will count against you as of right now. This was a shocking pronouncement given who His audience was. Those scribes and Pharisees who were trained scholars of the Torah were absolutely stunned. Never in the history of the world, and as far as they were concerned, never anywhere in scripture had any man ventured to say such a thing. No one before Jesus had ever assumed to have the authority to do such a thing as to forgive sins. That was something completely outside the range of human possibility and reserved solely for Jehovah Himself. Not one of the great patriarchs and revered Biblical characters from Moses on down did anything like that. What Jesus had done in their eyes was tantamount to blaspheme. Blaspheme is defined as to speak impiously or inappropriately about God. To defame, rail on, revile or speak evil of God is what it means, literally and specifically, as it relates to the disrespect of God's sacredness. This was one of the most serious of all sins anyone could commit –to dishonor God's exclusive position as God. Like in this case, He, Jesus, was basically saying that He was equal to God. To those religious leaders this was not even debatable.

This was one of the most basic of their teachings that every student learned from the very beginning. You should never say anything to suggest you are God. Jesus was fully aware of the reaction He was going to get from the scribes and the Pharisees. He knew these trained scholars were going to go off when He said this. This was just one of three occasions in the Bible when Jesus crossed that line. The other two incidences were when He preached His initial message in Nazareth where He grew up, after He read *Isaiah 61:1*; then, in the New Testament in *Luke 4:20-21*, Luke said Jesus closed the book and told them "This day is this scripture fulfilled in your ears." They got so worked up and agitated that Jesus miraculously walked through the midst of the crowd to safety. The other incident was in *John 8:54-56* when the Pharisees questioned whether Jesus was of God or not. When Jesus responded by saying that Abraham rejoiced to see His day, they told him they were of Abraham's seed. And they did not know where He was from. Jesus said, "Before Abraham was, I am." I am is the designation strictly reserved from God Himself. They literally took up stones to kill Jesus. This account is much like that, in that everyone in that room was filled with a sense of indignation and alarm that Jesus would say such a thing.

Given the beliefs and background of the people in that room and the purpose for why all the scribes and Pharisees had gathered in that house on that day, it was clear that Jesus was indeed trying to make a point. Jesus could have done this in a way where He did not offend or upset this crowd. If He wanted to heal this man, there was a way to do it wherein He would not have put Himself at odds with these religious experts. But Jesus intentionally was trying to get their attention, to make them aware of something they might never have ever thought of. He risked getting them all riled up in order to get them to see a significant point. That point being your mindset in ministry. Jesus was challenging their mindset in ministry. In other words when you do ministry, what is your objective or motivation? How do you use the scriptures to minister to people? Is your knowledge of the scriptures in any way beneficial to someone like this man suffering from a terminal disease? What, in your theology, is of any practical good for someone having a hard time? What is behind your thinking when you do ministry? He asked them a question when they thought He had blasphemed, "Why think ye evil in your hearts?" Why do you interpret something good like this man being healed, as something bad? When you are intent on looking for evil, you will see evil in everything. When you start off with a negative assumption, everything, even good things, will seem negative. The point Jesus was making is do not assume an evil disposition. Be open to God moving and believe for the best. How you think affects everything about you. Our mental health is the basis for our spiritual well-being. Without a strong mental base, our spiritual balance is very shaky. In the next chapter I want to emphasize the relationship between our mental and spiritual make-ups.

CHAPTER 4

YOUR MENTAL CAPACITY

Now *Proverbs 23:7* says, "As a man thinketh in his heart so is he…" Another way to put this is what you think is what you are. Notice it does not say as a man believes in his heart so is, he. The way you think dictates who you are. Of all the things you should be concerned about or on top of, that is of significance and important, is how you think because it affects you the most. What you think about, the way you process things in your mind, the depth of your thinking, and the quality of your thoughts, as well as the command you have over your thoughts, have a major impact on everything about you. You can be so sincere and have such deep needs. You can desire or want to do better and get delivered so much, but you cannot ever get any further than the kind of thinking going on in your head. It speaks to what life is all about. I dare say the kind of things going through your head have the greatest bearing on the kind of life you are living. In this study I want to suggest to you that Jesus came to save us from the wrong kind of thinking. The major thrust of the ministry of Jesus was aimed at getting us to think right. The biggest problem with sin and the effects of sin is how it messes up your thinking and causes your mind to take you down a self-destructive road. The bondage of sin exists in your mind and in your thinking. Your outward actions are the result of a corrupt mindset; inappropriate thoughts driving the mind to do and say things that are against you and take you away from God. Your freedom takes place when your way of thinking changes. It is not so much a religious thing as it is a mental transformation. Living in sin is living in bondage to a foreign, evil nature that controls your thinking. This is what keeps you from being free. Salvation is the introduction of a new way of thinking and consequently, allows you to live a new lifestyle.

When we look closely at what Jesus taught and what His ministry was all about, we realize the major emphasis was on our mental well-being. Our salvation is also being saved from mental instability or weakness. The teachings of Jesus Christ were aimed at building us up from within. It's about making us inwardly strong, secure and stable. The theology of the Apostle Paul was that salvation allows the believer to have power. This power is in the form of mental capacity to operate in supernatural ways. It is the mental capacity that was most affected by the fall of Adam. When you look at the results of Adam's sin in the garden, the worst effect was the loss of his power and the decline of his mental capacities. Consequently, it makes sense that the salvation Jesus brings to us is to restore power and mental capacity. What is it that we are saved from or what is it that we are saved to? Weren't we saved from a weak mental capacity and lack of power?

Let me define mental capacity. I believe mental capacity is the ability to maintain your balance and equilibrium in all situations. It has to do with your resiliency and durability. It is you being able to absorb adversity and misfortune. Being able to bounce back and never lose your place or position. It also relates to your thinking power in which you incorporate things, like your creativity and adaptability to change. It is also your mind being adept at knowing how to be resourceful and react to various things that come up; not losing your composure. Your mental capacity enables you to be in control of your inner faculties wherein you're able to execute under pressure with skill and proficiency. It has to do with your level of strength. It is your command over yourself.

I am astonished at how much of the ministry of Jesus was aimed at building up the mental capacity of those He ministered to. It led me to the conclusion that it is your mental capacity that is most affected by the experience of being saved. For example, Jesus said "…that men ought always to pray, and not to faint;"

Prayer enables you to withstand pressure without collapsing. When Jesus was talking about faith, wasn't He talking about mental strength? For example, when the disciples panicked in the storm and He asked them, where is their faith? Wasn't that about them losing heart and cracking under the pressure of the storm? Or what about when Peter saw the winds and the waves, and he cried out "LORD, save me!" Wasn't that a breakdown in their mental strength? Aren't these examples of faith being equated with mental strength? Or what about the feeding of the 5,000; wasn't Jesus testing their faith when He wanted them to exert their mental faculties to feed all those people? Instead of sending them away, He wanted them to use their mental faculties to feed the people.

Time and time again I have noticed that faith is associated with mental capacity. Abraham, in *Romans 4*, is said to have been strong in faith. What does it mean to be strong in faith? When you look closely in this Chapter, you will see it is the exercise of his mental faculties in the face of severe conflicting circumstances. "He staggered not at the promise of God through unbelief; but was strong in faith, giving glory to God." *Romans 4:20*. He was mentally firm when there was pressure to collapse or fall. Or what about the parable of the unjust judge? The widow wins over because the judge gets tired of her constant pressure. Jesus is making the point that faith is the exerting of mental pressure and not giving up.

This is important because when you square off against something, whatever it is a question of, who has the power to prevail? When you are in an adverse or an unfortunate situation and you are dealing with some opposition, some threat, some type of imminent danger, the result is determined by whether you are mentally strong enough to prevail over it. Faith allows you to overcome anything, withstand all things, win at all levels. On the reverse side, unbelief is the collapse of mental capacity. It is unbelief when you give up or quit. When you allow situations and circumstances to get to you to the point where you cave in, this is a lack of trust; this is unbelief. It is a lack of trust and unbelief when you throw in the towel. When you concede and surrender, you are letting everything go. Jesus told Peter "...and when thou art converted, strengthen thy brethren." Conversion or transformation is about being in a position where you don't collapse or you don't cave in or throw in the towel, but you are able to withstand adversity.

When Jesus told Jairus "Don't be afraid; just believe, and she will be healed", wasn't that about continuing to exercise his mental faculties despite the report from the house that his daughter was dead? And, what about the account of Lazarus, that they might believe? In these extreme situations, where it seemed undeniably impossible for them to believe; nevertheless, it was still possible if they only believed. Wasn't Jesus' confrontation with Martha about getting her to believe when she had clearly given up on her brother's life? When Paul says in Ephesians, "be strong in the Lord, and in the power of his might", isn't he talking about mental strength? Draw your strength from God. When James talks about "Knowing this, that the trying of your faith worketh patience"; isn't this mental strength or your mental capacity to withstand a lot and not break down?

Faith is associated with mental capacity. Your mental capacity is the evidence of your faith. Jesus associated the disciples' fear, anxiety and despair as an indication of their lack of faith. The change the Holy Spirit brings into our lives is that He gives us power and that power is mental capacity. There is a notable difference between the disciples before they received the Holy Spirit and after they were filled with the Holy Spirit. Peter stood up to the same ones, the disciples, that he feared and denied the Lord three times. Peter slept when he was supposed to be executed the next day (Acts 12) and James had already been executed. The Holy Spirit equips you to handle any kind of circumstance without breaking you down.

In spiritual warfare it is your mental strength that allows you to win. It's likened to a wrestling match where it is your will against the will of your opponent. Victory is outlasting the opposition. The reason why we win is because we have the mental strength and the mental capacity to endure and outlast the opposition. When our spiritual approach involves the proper emphasis on our mental constitution, then we are in position to foster strong faith.

CHAPTER 5

MY THINKING – AN ASSET OR LIABILITY?

Given what we have said about faith as being the result of a mental act, namely believing, the key becomes changing the way you think. It is about managing your thoughts and allowing your way of thinking to become an asset for you. Spirituality has more to do with your mind than it does with anything else. As a matter of fact, it is through the exercise of your thinking that really constitutes spiritual activity. Every spiritual faculty begins with some variations of exercising your mind.

This calls for a totally different orientation; a new way of looking at spiritual things, if you will. Particularly, in a specific situation, the emphasis is on the management of my thoughts as opposed to the management of the situation. We are suggesting that you look to your faith as the solution to the challenges you face. To walk by faith is to depend on faith. Faith is the source. For example, instead of focusing on what is against us, we focus on what we have available to us and for us in God's Word. We walk by faith and not by sight. While the natural inclination is to look for answers through your own physical senses, I am suggesting you look for answers through the exercising of your faith.

I am talking about the mind taking the central role in all spiritual actions. Peter says in his epistle "Wherefore gird up the loins of your mind" see *1 Peter 1:13a* and Paul tells us in *Romans 12:2* "And be not conformed to this world: but be ye transformed by the renewing of our mind." In *Romans 8:6-7* he says, "For to be carnally minded is death; but to be spiritually minded is life and peace. Because the carnal mind is enmity against God: for it is not subject to the law of God, neither indeed can be." Paul told Timothy, see 2 *Timothy 1:7* "For God hath not given us the spirit of fear; but of power, and of love, and of a sound mind." Engaging your mind in spiritual thinking constitutes the answer to handling a situation.

Thinking in the way to believe is the most significant spiritual activity you can develop. Believing is the difference between something being carnal or that something being spiritual. It is the difference between something being of God and something not of God. Without believing, whatever you do is just a religious act. When you believe, it becomes a spiritual act.

When you understand that believing is to think something to be true, then you realize any time you want to do anything spiritual it starts with your thinking. Thinking in a way that your thoughts are aligned with the truth of God's Word is to engage in spiritual thinking. We are not talking about letting your mind wander but setting your thinking on spiritual things. Being intentional about what you set your thinking on as the reality of what you are focused on. Do not allow your mind to get entangled by the wrong type of thoughts. Make sure your thinking is free from doubts and free from false assumptions or negative conclusions. It is so important in keeping your mind clear from conflicting thoughts and evil imaginations. You must be alert and attentive to any kind of mental blockage or flawed thinking. You must be free from double-mindedness and wavering back and forth. Distractions are a major issue. You must stay focused on the Word of God.

Believing is the single most important thing you can do. It is the most impactful activity in your life. Believing is how we gain access to the unlimited resources of God. What you believe dictates everything about who you are. Believing sets the parameters for what you can become. If there is one thing Jesus emphasized to His disciples more than anything else, it was the necessity of believing. In just about every instance the point of the account was to emphasize the need to believe.

Believing is how you overcome adversity. Believing is your

response to attacks. Believing is what you do when you experience misfortune. Sometimes it is not clear why something happened. There are times when you cannot necessarily see how something is going to turn out. A lot of times you don't know exactly what God is doing. You don't know how He is going to move. But the one thing you must do every time, and in every instance, you must believe.

Let me take a moment and describe just exactly what believing is. Believing is the disposition of your thinking. It is how you choose to process what you think. To believe is to set a positive tone to what you think about. Believing is how you think. This means to put your thoughts and thinking in a precise context. That context is a context in which you are believing. It is like you connect your thoughts so that they are all moving in a specific, precise direction.

There is this process where your thoughts are made to contribute to a particular purpose or goal. All thinking is to be believing. You are to believe all the time. At no point are you ever to approach anything without believing. You don't start believing when something happens; you believe so that you are already believing when things do happen. You are not supposed to overreact to situations. If you are believing you will not overreact because believing equips you to keep your composure. Your belief makes you flexible to change, resilient to misfortune, calm in the midst of a trial or storm, and when life brings challenges. When you are believing, your mind keeps thinking and keeps you in command of your situation.

If you are believing, then your mind remains active and working continuously, on your behalf. Believing is the act of exercising your mind in a precise direction. Believing is the main thing the enemy does not want you to do. He aims every one of his strategies toward you to get you or keep you in unbelief.

God's Word has already been made available and it is ready to come to pass; however, believing is the way it becomes a transaction that goes into effect. It is like a formula that needs all the elements to be in place: You need God's Word and your belief for things to happen on your behalf. Jesus told Martha, "if you can believe you can see the glory of God." Jesus said, "...If ye have faith as a grain of mustard seed..." *Matthew 17:20*

I love the account in Luke 5 where the room was full of people and Luke tells us that "...the power of the Lord was present to heal them." But no one was believing so nothing was happening. When Jesus went to His hometown to preach, despite being filled with the power without measure, He could there do no mighty work among them except heal a few sick people. He marveled at their unbelief. Jesus said in *Mark 11:24*, "...What things soever ye desire, when ye pray, believe that ye receive them, and ye shall have them."

How many things has God spoken in His Word that cannot come to pass because you have not yet believed those things to be true? Instances in the Bible where people were promised things and they did not come to pass for them was always because of one thing –they failed to believe. This explains why the enemy always focuses on your thinking to stop you from believing and receiving. He knows he cannot stop God's Word and so his emphasis is on what you might believe. The scripture calls his power the power of darkness. Darkness is associated with confusion or lack of clarity of vision. The enemy's power is to cloud the truth and keep you unaware of the reality of God's Word. *Hosea 4:6a* says, "My people are destroyed for lack of knowledge..." *Matthew 8:13* says "...and as thou hast believed, so be it done unto thee..." In other words, you can receive in proportion to what you believe. As much as you believe is as much as you will have available for yourself or for you to receive. God can bless your way beyond your need; however, what you believe determines just how much you will receive –this is the believing element. It is not a question of whether God can give you enough –it is always a question as to how much you can believe for. He told Bartimaeus in *Luke 18:42*, "...Receive thy sight: thy faith hath saved thee." He attributed his healing to be his faith. He told the woman with the issue of blood, "...Daughter, be of good comfort: thy faith hath made thee whole; go in peace." *Luke 8:48*

Let me share some more insights on what it means to believe.

To believe is to aim your thoughts, particularly in a specific direction. Believing is targeting some particular outcome based on the Word of God. To believe is to apply specific scriptures from God's Word to yourself. God's Word is for the whosoever – it is for anyone, but it is not applicable to you until you believe it. Believing is the equivalent of personalizing scriptures from God's Word for you, personally. You make the scriptures your scriptures from God's Word.

Another way to see this is to take possession of specific scriptures from the Word –as if to make them yours. You establish ownership of those scriptures as belonging to you. Still another aspect to believing is that you accept specific scriptures from the Word as being true for you in your situation. Instead of thinking some other reality, you choose to think of the scriptures from the Word as being your truth for you. You receive, believe and agree with what God's Word says as having the final authority and the truest of reality, that is, what you declare to be true.

To believe is to position yourself in proximity to the Word of God where it's your source, and from this source only you receive. As opposed to looking within yourself or trying to do things on your own, believing is drawing from the Word as the means by which you respond to a situation.

To believe is to adopt, particularly, a point of view that is according to God's Word. When you believe, you assume something is true and at the same time assume something else is not going to be true for you. The act of believing is at the same time the act of disbelieving something that conflicts with the Word of God.

To believe God's Word means you're going to think and believe as God's written Word has stated, nothing else. You are literally deciding to take what God has said as authoritative over anything else that may be out there. To believe is to direct your thinking in line with God's Word. You exercise your mind in a way where you use your thoughts to reinforce what God's Word says. Essentially, you set your thinking, particularly, in a way where everything must adhere to the Word of God.

To believe is to actively take command of your thoughts and make yourself think in a specific way. When Jesus told Jairus to "believe only" He was commanding him to not think anything other than the reality, that his daughter would be made whole.

Another aspect to your believing is to look or expect things to happen according to the Word which God has spoken. Expectation is critical to believing because your expectation is the motivation for believing. Believing is to think in ways that are only in agreement or in line with what God's Word says. Believing is not just a one-time thing that happens when you initially believe. It is an on-going and continual process.

To believe is to allow yourself to think beyond what your senses dictate or discern, or even your mind can reason. Believing is not limited to what is visible but it allows you to access that which is invisible. Believing is to use your mind to explore possibilities beyond the scope of human capability or ability. To believe is to tap into the unlimited capacity of God's Word to cause things to happen on your behalf. To believe is to trust what God has said over and above anything that is possible for you to accomplish on your own. Believing is the main thing we must do as Christians. Now, since believing is thinking, I thought it would be necessary to talk some more about what it really means to think. We will cover more on this in our next chapter.

CHAPTER 6

TO THINK

Since believing involves thinking let me share some insights on what it means to think. To think is to make yourself conscious of the spiritual reality or truth. It is also to focus your mind particularly on something specific. To think is to make a choice about what you deem as true, as opposed to something else you determine to not be true. It is also to look closely at or seek to understand something in terms of its significance or meaning.

Now, there are some things you don't want to do concerning your thinking. First, you don't want to think on the wrong things. Second, in some cases, you don't want to think at all about certain things. And third, you don't want to think about two conflicting things at once. That is called being double-minded.

Now, you may ask, aren't there some disconcerting things that can happen when you think about something too much? Yes. First, you can magnify it and make it greater than it is. In addition to that, when you think too much you distract yourself and literally weaken your faith –your mindset. When you think too much or overly think, you focus on things that reduce your faith and highlight your human frailty. It causes you to lose your mental intensity and passion when you think too much, which is why one of the commandments was given in the Old Testament — that of keeping the Sabbath. God recognized the need for rest. This was a way to provide a diversion and refresh the mind.

You may also ask, why is what you think about so important?

It determines your mindset. It is the way you manage your mindset. Your mindset is a direct result of what you choose to think about. How much faith you have is directly related to what you have been thinking about. Did you know that whatever you think about determines the direction of your life? What you think about determines what you can or cannot do. It is what determines your access to God and the quality of your connection with Him. I would even say whatever you think about determines your sense of well-being. How you feel about yourself and others is the result of what you think about. Most importantly, whatever you think about is how you assess your situation or condition.

Why is your level of thinking so important? First, you cannot rise beyond your level of thinking. Your capacity to perform anything is connected to your level of thinking. If you think you cannot do something, you are severely hampered in any attempts to do just that. Another way that your thinking affects you is in what you can or cannot perceive as reality. When you have a specific way of thinking it affects how you see things. You look at things through the lenses of how you think about those things. It is like your mind focuses on certain aspects of something because there is a preconceived notion about what it is. Consequently, there comes an ignoring of other aspects because the mind has deemed those characteristics or aspects not significant.

The view you have of your life challenges and experiences is another aspect that is affected by your thinking. An experience can either be positive or negative, depending on how you process it. Sometimes, it's sad and unfortunate, that even the good things God can do for us can be misconstrued and be interpreted as something negative. This is what happened in the wilderness with the children of Israel. Despite all the blessings they received from God during their time in the wilderness, they could never accept the things God did for them as good. Eventually God announces in *Hebrews 3:10*, "Wherefore I was grieved with that generation, and said, "...They do alway err in their heart; and they have not known my ways." They always assumed the worst about everything He did for them. Their experience was affected by their flawed way of thinking.

Overall, your quality of life is dictated to you by how you

think. Your ability to enjoy life is tied to how you think. When Jesus said, "...I am come that they might have life, and that they might have it more abundantly." I believe Jesus came to show us a way to have a better quality of life. That includes showing us how to think. You can have material possessions, but material possessions cannot satisfy you. When you are full of insecurities, turmoil and confusion, all the material wealth in the world cannot help you to have a good quality of life. At the same time, you can have so little of material and possessions, if anything, but when your thinking is connected to God your life can be so great.

The greatest hindrance to a healthy relationship is the way the individuals think in that relationship. It is the single, greatest factor in terms of your capacity to overcome challenges. The way you think shapes how free you are. It affects your capacity to operate freely.

THE VALUE OF GOD'S WORD

The Word of God is the key to quality thinking. The Word of God enables you to have something to think about in every kind of situation. Not only that but God's Word gives you the answer to any dilemma you will encounter. It is the Word of God that is the empowering force that keeps your faith strong and effective.

This act of believing generates power on the inside. This power is aimed at things you are thinking about. There is power in the thinking process. The truth makes what you think powerful. This power that emanates from you is faith. Consequently, you have a mindset that allows you to tap into the realm of the Spirit. It gives you access to the unlimited resources of God.

This power generated on the inside of you is the result of your thinking. It is managed by the degree to which you can maintain a disciplined mind on the truth. The way this works is that situations will arise, and in response to those situations, your thinking will be thrown off. This distracted thinking can reduce the power generated by your belief of what you thought to be true. Again, the key to keeping this power generated and working is maintaining your thinking on what is true. This power on the inside of you cannot only keep you straight but can be released in a way where you impact the situations you face. This faith can produce healings in you and in the lives of others. It can cause things to change for the better.

You are responsible for how much power you have on the inside of you. Your thoughts are carriers of energy. When you think things according to God's Word there is power released by those thoughts. By power being released, I mean, literally, that there is energy emanating from you affecting the things you are thinking about. There are literally vibes being released that are affecting other people associated with those thoughts. In some cases, people are feeling things from the vibes coming from you when you are having those thoughts.

As you think these thoughts according to God's Word there is life communicated or transferred to people around you. There is literally a boost of energy they feel by just your mere presence. People are put at ease because they feel the zest for life energy radiating from you. In some cases, that zest for life energy coming from you can cause people to become both encouraged and more confident about life. It is as if your mindset travels to other people and they are affected by the mindset you have. People become inspired by the zest of energy you give off. As you think God's thoughts, there is activation of inner potency and capacity. Your entire being starts to respond to what you are thinking about, accordingly, on the Word of God. For example, your mind begins to manufacture creative thoughts and recalls pertinent information. It starts to focus on the spiritual reality causing the effects of distracting, negative and weakening information to cease. Your emotions come in line with this line of thinking. You start to feel what is compatible with what you are thinking. For example, you literally feel calm, confident and at peace. Your desires are triggered so that you start to crave spiritual things as opposed to carnal things. You want to pray. You want to worship. You want to love God and serve others. Even your physical body is affected by what you are thinking. Fatigue is the result of exerting a lot of mental energy that drains a person after a while. It has been proven that stress weakens the immune system, making you more susceptible to illnesses and disease. It is almost as if your body reacts to negative thoughts by starting to malfunction. Your heart rate and even your blood pressure rises, and your breathing becomes challenged, along with many other physical reactions. When you constantly think on God's Word, literally, mental energy, which has the effect of activating good emotions like joy, excitement and pleasure, are activated. Nothing is healthier than to think on God's Word. It has the most therapeutic effect on you, both mentally and physically. Thinking on God's Word lifts you up, internally, to a place where your spiritual senses start to provide spiritual information. You perceive spiritual reality. This has the effect of increasing your mindset and your faith. You become more convinced, more confident and locked into a faith-mindset. Your faith, which comes in quantities, will grow and expand in its influences on you, your situation and on others. Power is increasingly emanating from you. Instead of an on-going situation wearing you down over time, the faith-mindset grows inside you, causing you to get stronger and more capable over time. It is as if you have this inner source that is supplying you, fortifying you and keeping you fresh during the entire ordeal. As a matter of fact, instead of wishing, hoping and praying that things were over and desiring for things to come to an end, you will enjoy the application of your faith while anticipating all that God is going to do through the situation. This all happens as you think according to God's Word and when you make God's Word the object of your thinking. You enable your mind to become an asset, rather than a liability. You make your thinking an instrument for good as opposed to binding and limiting. You make thoughts work for you, releasing energy and vitality. You make yourself capable, equipped and strong by thinking according to God's Word.

There are three ways your thinking can throw you off and, consequently, cause you to not have enough faith. First, your thinking can literally be turned off; you do not think something to be true or believe the situation, and for whatever other reasons, you simply do not believe in the face of the specific situation.

Another way is that your thinking can inhibit your faith when your thinking is on two things all at once. There are competing thoughts going on in your mind. This is when you are thinking about something that is true and something that is untrue, both at the same time. James calls this double minded. When you are double minded you cannot receive anything of the Lord.

And thirdly, you can be thinking on the wrong things. You are focused on things other than the truth of God's Word. The spiritual reality of God's truth is not what you are thinking about –you could be thinking about some other reality. However, in all these three cases, these types of thinking can cause you to operate in unbelief. To believe is to think something to be true. That means distractions are the major problem. A distraction's power is in its ability to get you to think on it. It, of itself, cannot do you any harm, but its power is getting you to think about it. Great faith comes from great focus because energy is released when you think about the right things. Energy is lost when you think about the wrong things. The sheer thinking on a distraction is enough to upset your faith. Putting on the whole armor of God and thinking on the fruits of the Spirit are all right ways of thinking. The enemy is a distractor but when you can stay focused on what the Word of God says belongs to you, you will not waver in your faith.

One of the things that is clear from the Mueller Report is that the 2016 Election of the United States was attacked by the Russian Government. It was not an attack with missiles, bullets and bombs. It was something much more powerful – information. It was a massive misinformation campaign aimed at disrupting and destabilizing our system of democracy. They succeeded in their goal of helping to get the candidate they wanted elected by using false information to divide the country. Posing as various groups they were able to use social media and the news media, in general, to suppress certain voting blocs or alliances by mobilizing others. Even after this was proven to be what happened, there is still some doubts or questions as to whether the appropriate steps have since been taken to prevent this from happening again in the future. This is a direct page out of the book of Satan himself. Spreading misinformation is the nature of his work; the battle for truth is the spiritual battle. The struggle has always been between good and evil. Evil has always operated in misinformation and good operates in the truth. Truth is the most powerful force in the world. It is no wonder that his reign is the kingdom of darkness; darkness because his aim is to conceal, hide and distract from the truth. Truth represents light and clarity.

The focal point of his campaign is for the minds of people. Our struggle is for truth. Jesus is the way, the truth and the life. In the prophecy of Hosea, it says, "My people are destroyed for lack of knowledge…" In Timothy, Paul describes the house of God as "…the pillar and ground of the truth." *1 Timothy 3:15b.* He describes God's purpose, "Who will have all men to be saved, and to come unto the knowledge of the truth." *1 Timothy 2:4.*

He says the goal of studying is that you "Study to shew thyself approved unto God, a workman that needeth not to be ashamed, rightly dividing the word of truth." (2 Timothy 2:15) In *Ephesians 6:14*, he also stated "…having your loins girt about with truth…"

Truth is so important because it is the real reality. When you are believing something that is false your mind is disconnected from God's Word. God's Word is the source of everything. You can't receive anything when you are not drawing from a legitimate source like the Word of God. The truth is compatible with God and whenever you are not in the truth you are not capable of relating to God.

If believing is thinking that which is true, unbelieving is thinking something that is not true. Believing can operate in the reverse. Believing in something that is true can benefit you greatly. Consequently, believing in something that is not true can do you a lot of harm. When something false occupies your mind, it prevents you from believing in the truth. That puts you in jeopardy of the negative effect of the false information and keeps you from getting what you need from the truth.

The level of truth you walk in determines the level of faith you can have. Since truth makes you free, bondage is the result of the failure to have truth. Truth is what makes the Word of God so liberating when it is believed. Truth fits you. You know it is the truth because it is of the same essence as God. This is so important because if something is not the truth, it cannot help you.

The most powerful thing you can do is think the truth. Where you apply your mental energy is where your power is going. Don't waste your mental energy on the wrong things. Don't use your mental energy for the wrong purposes or for the wrong reasons. Don't turn your mental energy on yourself. The power of God's Word is accessed when you think about or meditate on it, specifically; you cannot believe certain things when you think a specific way. Your thoughts get in the way of your beliefs. The number one hindrance to believing is how you think.

When you realize that faith is a mindset then you understand that different types of thinking are different ways of believing. Any type of thinking becomes important because it will either contribute to your mindset or it will diminish from your mindset. Memories are important, and how you store things in your mind have a tremendous impact on your mindset. Imagination is important because it affects the mind.

Focus is so important because it is critical to the mind. Any kind of thinking is either powerful or weakening. Thoughts are carriers of energy. Bad thoughts carry negative energy and good thoughts carry positive energy. Negative energy weakens you or lessens your mindset. Positive energy strengthens and increases your mindset. When you think good thoughts, your mindset is reinforced.

FAITH IS A MINDSET

The stronger your mindset the more power that emanates from you. The more resistant you are to doubt, the greater your optimism; the more secure your confidence, the more zip in your step; the more swag in your disposition, the more comfortable you are in your own skin; the more peace you are within yourself, the less threatened you are by other people; the more secure you are in who you are, the more assured you are in your ability; the better equipped you are for changes, the less vulnerable you are to be attacked, the more credible you are to yourself, the more creative you are in your thinking; the more upbeat you are about your chances, the more at ease you are about your situation; the higher hopes, the clearer your perspective; the greater your potential, the more joy in your heart; the higher your ceiling, the firmer your convictions; the more sound your discipline, the clearer your perspective; your healthy state of being, clarity of your vision and most of all, the stronger your beliefs.

Faith is a mindset. Walking by faith is to have a mindset that dominates your thinking. Exercising faith is employing a mindset in every situation you encounter in life. This faith mindset must be fed by the Word of God. It is strengthened by your belief in the Word of God. It is reinforced by meditation and concentration on God's Word. It is maintained by the management of your thinking in a way where the Word of God is the standard for any kind of thinking. There is this process going on of casting down imaginations and every high thing that would exalt itself against the knowledge of God and bringing into captivity every thought to the obedience of Christ. This mindset is grounded in the truth of God's Word and the liberating effect of the truth. It is empowered by the transmission of truth by way of the Holy Spirit — who is the Spirit of truth.

As the Holy Spirit reveals truth, the mind grasps the spiritual reality in the form of understanding. Understanding births creativity and discretion in the form of wisdom. Wisdom connects our minds to God's voice and His leading so that we are walking in the light or illumination of God's presence. This allows us to be in command of every situation, be equipped for anything that happens and we can be aware of whatever we need to know. We can be conscious of what is significant in every circumstance and energized by the hope and optimism caused by the constant flow of revelations in God's Word.

What you are thinking about is the most important factor in

any situation. Your faith is dependent on whether your thinking is contributing to or strengthening your mindset. The power that is being exercised against you is in the form of getting you to accept some way of thinking that can weaken you. It really is not about your circumstances as much as it is about how you interpret those circumstances. It is more about you assuming a way of thinking in which you concede, accept or give in to how your situation may appear to be.

Anything that you think is greater than you – you will make it greater than you. Anything you think or assume you cannot do –you cannot do. Anything you think is impossible –will be impossible for you. Anything in the negative sense you think will happen –you have no power to stop it from happening. Anything you become convinced of that is true, you can't deny or prevent from affecting you in some way.

A trial or a crisis always exposes how you think. It brings to light what you are thinking about. There is something about external pressure and inner turmoil that forces you to come to grips with what it is you constantly think about. Especially what and how you think and view God, which is why God uses trials to introduce Himself to you. He works in our lives in such a way as to introduce us to Him. He uses the situations you go through to teach you about Him and to get you to particularly, think a specific way about Him. For example, if God is going to be the center of your thinking, you must be made aware of how much you need Him. It's like you must come to a place of helplessness to really think of God as the only one who can help you. In *Psalms 121:2*, when David said, "My help cometh from the Lord..." that was something he learned from being in some helpless situations. You think about God differently when you have experienced some things and then you become keenly aware of just how little you could do on your own.

Spiritual growth has everything to do with advanced thinking.

You process things in a way in which God is the center of your assumptions and your conclusions about things. He becomes the center of your beliefs and expectations. You literally are as strong as your thinking. God wants you to have a perspective on things in that what you know about God affects how you view things. Learning about God changes how you think about everything. When you have the knowledge of God, this increases your thinking and you become influential, powerful and impactful.

Believers are thinkers and the degree to which you think dictates how much you can believe. You have as much potential as the quality of your thinking. Whenever God intends to do more through you, the first thing He does is raise your level of thinking. Your level of thinking determines what is possible for you.

There is a direct correlation between how you think and what you are capable of. Whenever you find people who cannot do what they need to do, it is always because they cannot, for whatever reason, think the way they should think.

How you think is your mentality. By mentality I mean the posture of your thinking, that is what you assume about yourself and what you assume about the situation. These are all products of what type of mentality you have. For example, you can have a winning mentality, or you can have a losing mentality, and consequently, whatever you think is shaped by whatever type of mentality you have. Webster's Dictionary defines mentality as mental power/capacity; mode or way of thought, way of thinking; your outlook. It is the sum of a person's intellectual capabilities or endowment.

Your mentality dictates what you think, and what you think is reflective of whatever that mentality is. Particularly, for example, when you have a specific mentality you perceive things a certain way. Joshua and Caleb saw things completely different from the way the other ten spies saw the situation because their mentality was different. They saw the Canaanites as prey, but the other spies saw them as giants.

It is always apparent what kind of mentality you have in a specific situation by what and how you think about the situation. When you have the wrong mentality, it does not matter whatever else you may have going for you, your mentality will ultimately dictate your fate. You can have so much talent and ability but without the right mentality your talent and ability will simply be wasted. God gave you His Word to feed your mentality. God does not promise you things so that you can do those things or make those things happen. Whatever God promises is an announcement of what He is going to do. The reason why He announces it to you is so that you can have the right mentality. It is not because He is in any way dependent on you to make it happen. Your job is believing it or maintaining your mentality while He does all the work.

Mentality is the disposition of your mind. It is not just what you think but how you think. It is your frame of mind or outlook. It is your mind-set, your view, your perspective on things. It is your mental state of being. It reveals that you do have an opinion on some things — how you think about everything. It is the most spiritual thing about you. It is the most carnal thing about you because whatever your mentality dictates to you, your capacity is to either relate it to God or not. If your mentality does not match what you intend to do, you will inevitably fail.

Many of the things Jesus spoke about in the Bible spoke to the type of mentality we are supposed to have. It is how you are to think about things, how you are to approach things. He said things like "...If thou canst believe, all things are possible to him that believeth." *Mark 9:23* "Ye are of God, little children, and have overcome them: because greater is he that is in you, than he that is in the world." *1 John 4:4* "...If ye have faith as a grain of mustard seed..." *Matthew 17:20.* Paul's teachings were about mentality. "I can do all things through Christ which strengthens me." *Philippians 4:13.* "Who shall separate us from the love of Christ?" *Romans 8:35; 37* "Nay, in all these things we are more than conquerors through him that loved us."

CHAPTER 7

IT'S ALL ABOUT THE WAY YOU THINK

When you realize it's all about thinking, it simplifies things a little better. You understand that the main thing you must do is to concentrate on this one thing, then you always know where to start. You start with your thinking. You can literally reverse any downward trend by thinking a different way. You can overcome any difficulty by raising your thinking above your circumstances. You can change how you process things and neutralize the effect certain things have on you. By employing the right kind of thinking, you can literally improve the quality of your life. Your thinking can put you at ease and give you a new lease on life. You can enjoy things that used to be unpleasant; do things you never thought you could do before. You can even live better than you even knew was possible by simply changing the way you think.

Paul tells us in Romans 12 that transformation takes place as a result of a renewed mind, and in Proverbs 23 Solomon tells us "For as he thinketh in his heart, so is he…" You could argue that the ministry of Jesus was about changing how mankind thinks –about everything. That is why the medium of change is the Word of God that must be applied to our minds. Spirituality begins with how you think. The difference in the spirituality of Jesus and the spirituality of the Pharisees was how they thought. The Pharisees thought the outward actions made them spiritual, but Jesus made it clear that the problem was that their thinking was flawed. Jesus said in *Matthew 15:8* "This people draweth nigh unto me with their mouth, and honoureth me with their lips; but their heart is far from me." They had the impressive outward act, but they lacked the appropriate inner motive. That is why Jesus said in the Beatitudes, *Matthew 5:8* "Blessed are the pure in heart for they shall see God." You can certainly do some things which appear, on the surface, to be righteous and devout, however, what is important to God is what's your motive and your way of thinking. Jesus said, the Pharisees did what they did to get the praise of men and, consequently, got their reward from the attention and acclaim of people, but God was not impressed or pleased at all by all they did. You remember when Jesus and the disciples were watching people put their money in the offering and this Pharisee came and gave this large sum of money, well everyone made a big ado. And then this widow came in and gave two mites. Jesus told His disciples the widow was more acceptable to God because the Pharisee gave for show and out of his abundance, but the widow gave all she had. Worship is not your physical posture or emotional display; true worship is what is going on in your mind and the kind of interaction you are having with God in your heart. You can be physically prostrate on the ground but absolute defiant and rebellious in your mind.

As I said earlier, everything becomes simpler when you realize how important it is for you to manage your thinking. Your power is in your thoughts. All bondage exists in your mind and must be addressed by a change in your thinking. The truth must be applied to your mind for you to be free. You are as healthy as your thinking is appropriate. The strategy of the enemy is always the same — get you to think the wrong kind of thoughts. You are as strong as your mind is operating in the truth. Truth, meaning the accurate, right representation of reality is what keeps us from becoming entangled in our minds. Your capacity is tied to the quality of your thinking. You have a greater potential as you apply your thinking in the right way. Conversion is first and foremost a change in your thinking. Salvation occurs only after a change has taken place in your mind. You are as saved as your thinking has aligned itself to God. Consequently, you can never rise higher than the level of your thinking. You cannot be delivered beyond a change in your thinking.

Your thinking drives everything. It is the root and origin of all unbelief, all weaknesses and every kind of affliction. Your thinking is behind all failure, defeat and powerlessness. You can trace sin, wickedness and eventual death to ungodly ways of thinking. Paul said "For to be carnally minded is death; but to be spiritually minded is life and peace. *Romans 8:6*

When a believer loses their way, it started with them thinking in the wrong way. Any time someone turns from God it starts with them thinking differently. It is the single greatest factor in your resiliency. It has the greatest impact on the outcome of things –how you think.

Faith is a word that straddles the realm of the Spirit and the natural world. There are some words that do that because you cannot define them with human or natural terms. All you can do is describe them or say what they are like because there is nothing in the natural realm like it. One word cannot define it, you must obtain a combination of words and terms to even describe what it is like. It's like when Jesus was talking to Nicodemus about being born again and Jesus told him "That which is born of the flesh is flesh; and that which is born of the Spirit is spirit." *John 3:6*. Or when Paul said in *1 Corinthians 2:14*, "But the natural man receiveth not the things of the Spirit of God: for they are foolishness unto him: neither can he know them, because they are spiritually discerned." For example, can anyone define glory? There is no human definition for glory because it is something that is from the realm of God. When Moses asked to see His glory what was he asking for? Also, the word holy is another example. God is holy and there is nothing in the natural that can explain what holy means. Another thing about these types of terms is that they can only be experienced and not fully understood. You know they are real because you experience them, but you cannot find words to describe them because there are no words for them in the natural.

Faith is this way in that no one term can define it and no group of terms can fully describe it, and yet, it is so real and unmistakable in terms of effect. Faith is a force in the earth, and it has the greatest bearing on your well-being. Faith releases power. There are some things which happened in my life and I have no idea how I got from point A to point B; all I know is that I believed, and things happened.

There is a direct relationship between faith and power. Faith literally sets things in motion. Faith releases energy into the atmosphere. Faith dispatches angels. Faith literally makes things happen. Faith causes things to change. When you have faith, situations around you move to their proper place. Faith takes you beyond human limitations. Faith can do things that are beyond your human ability. For example, faith can travel millions of miles away and affect things long into your future. You can believe something today and it can impact future generations long after you are gone. As a matter of fact, faith is not at all limited by space or time. There is no distance too great for your faith or anything too far for your faith to reach. Right now, you have been impacted by the faith that was exercised by someone long ago. You are benefiting from some things people who believed before you were even born. It was their faith which explains how certain things have happened or turned out for you.

When you realize everything is affected by your faith, then you will focus on it more than anything else. However, you must ensure that whatever you do, you will keep your faith intact. Never allow anything to cause you to lose your faith. Do not ever become distracted by anything that could make you stop exercising your faith. Under no circumstances or any conditions are you to ever doubt, overreact or concede defeat, and never assume the worst or panic.

In the face of an adverse situation, concentrate on one thing –keeping your faith strong. You must manage yourself by managing your faith. A lot may be going on around you but make sure your faith does not waver, shrink or decline. You can win, so long as you have faith. There is hope, so long as you still have your faith. The odds may be against you, but your faith gives you the best chance to win. "… and this is the victory that overcometh the world, even our faith." *1 John 5:4*. It is the single greatest variable in whether, or not, good things are coming to you.

Your faith is doing things that are not visible to your eyes. Your faith is moving things around and changing things in your favor.

Your faith is giving off vibes, causing things to happen. Faith is something that literally emanates from you, goes out from you, and makes things happen. Jesus said faith was a force. It is a power that could do things like cause a fig tree to dry up and cause a mountain to be removed and be cast into the sea.

Faith allows you to be at ease because it is taking care of some things, as opposed to you trying to take care of them on your own. People who have faith understand it is not them making things happen; it is their faith that causes things to happen. That means people who have faith are not at all stressed out. They are not feeling pressure to make things happen. People with faith are not concerned about their ability or their resources. They are not depending on their knowledge of something or their physical strength. People with faith know it is their faith that is going to make things happen.

Jesus models for us how it is to live by faith because He, at no time, ever displayed anxiety about what He was doing. At no time did He ever show any concern about the way things appeared or what He had to do. It almost seems like Jesus was oblivious to outward circumstances because He modeled for us the fact that when you live by faith it does not matter what things look like. It does not matter what is going on around you; your faith is all you are to think about.

For example, Jesus is sleeping through a major, violent storm. He is fast asleep. The disciples are trying to keep the water out of the boat to prevent the boat from sinking. They are trying to make sure that the boat does not tip over as it is being impacted by the wind and the waves. They are struggling and wrestling with these circumstances which appeared to be getting worse by the minute. And yet Jesus is fast asleep. The disciples decide to wake Him up. They are literally frustrated when they say to Him, "...Master, carest thou not that we perish?" *Mark 4:38* And yet, Jesus does not show any degree of panic or even concern; He merely gets up and rebukes the wind and waves and says "Peace, be still." Then He turns to them and ask them, "...Why are ye so fearful? how is it that ye have no faith?" Now, this is not about the intensity or danger of the storm; it is about the fact that the disciples failed to exercise their faith.

The entire situation of feeding the 5,000 was all about modeling for them how they were to think. Jesus was teaching them about having faith in a challenging situation. The disciples assumed they were in a no-win situation. It was late in the evening and the people had been out there in a desert-like place all day. It was a health crisis because under that hot subtropical sun, dehydration was a real possibility, along with the fact that they had not eaten anything all day. They were in a place where there was no available food or water, and if something happened, it would be a public-relations nightmare because they were out there listening to Jesus preach. The disciples thought it was necessary to get Jesus to send the crowd away even though they conceded that some of them were probably going to faint on their way home. Jesus, much like in the case of the storm, seems to be on a totally different wavelength than the disciples. He says to them "You give them something to eat." *Matthew 14:16*. I am sure they were looking at Him saying, what in the world! Give them something to eat! Then He asked them what do you have available to feed the people with? This was a challenge for them to think in positive ways. Don't concede to a situation –use your faith.

The raising of Lazarus from the dead was about teaching them about faith. Living by faith is a good way to live; it is a way to do things and get things accomplished. It is an attitude you must have about things. It is the way that you think. Faith is the way you react to situations. It is the way you take on challenges. Faith is a way to win. It is a way to overcome things. Faith is the way we relate to God. It is the way we process everything going on around us. The Bible says "…The just shall live by faith…" *Romans 1:17a*. Also, the Bible says on faith, "But without faith it is impossible to please him: for he that cometh to God must believe that he is, and that he is a rewarder of them that diligently seek him." *Hebrews 11:6*

CHAPTER 8

THE INTERCHANGE BETWEEN SPIRIT, SOUL AND BODY

We are a spirit. We have a soul. We live inside a body. The three aspects of our being are spirit, soul and body. In times past, I always taught that these three aspects of our being were separate and distinct, however, I now believe these three aspects of our being co-exist together; there is considerable interchange and an overlap in function and purpose. For example, it is well documented that there is a link between mental health and physical health. Studies have shown that stress weakens the immune system, making people more susceptible to disease. Many doctors acknowledge that 80% of symptoms patients complain about in doctors' offices are what they call psychosomatic.

Medical researchers who study brain activity found that those patients who prayed or engaged in worship showed noticeable improvement in their recovery, compared to those who did not. When they studied this, the brain triggered areas of those spiritual activities mentioned and they found that those areas were the ones associated with feelings of euphoria and peace. All of this points to what I like to call "the overlap" between these two areas.

I have always taught that the soul is the mind, will and emotions. I used to think what I thought, what I felt and what I desired were from the soulish realm. This realm, I thought, was separate from the spirit. As a matter of fact, I used to teach that you had to feed the spirit so that it could exert control over the mind, will and emotions. When you could not resist temptation for example, I would say that was because you did not feed your spirit enough to be able to overpower your flesh. I even used to advocate that scripture in the Garden of Gethsemane where Jesus told the disciples, "...the spirit indeed is willing, but the flesh is weak." *Matthew 26:41b*. When Jesus said the spirit indeed is willing, but the flesh is weak, He was not suggesting some separation, but rather emphasizing the opposite in that you have to impose your will on your flesh and choose to follow the leading of the Spirit.

Your spirit is not an independent faculty but rather, your spirit is tied to your mental and physical being. Jesus wanted them to pray and not fall to sleep. Prayer is not your spirit taking over you but rather the engagement of your mind and will to exercise yourself in a spiritual activity. Spiritual activity cannot happen without your mind, will and emotions, which is why Paul says in *1 Timothy 4:7b*, "exercise thyself rather unto godliness." "For bodily exercise profiteth little: but godliness is profitable unto all things, having promise of the life that now is, and of that which is to come." *1 Timothy 4:8* Clearly Paul is talking about the action of spiritual activity being the result of mental action. There is a lot of theology out there that suggests that the Spirit operates on His own. People sing that song, "Every time I feel the spirit moving in my heart, I will pray." If you are waiting around to feel something before you pray, then you might never pray. I would suggest that the best time to pray may be when you feel nothing.

It does not make sense that you could have your spirit doing something and your mind, will or emotions are not involved. It is like your spirit is operating on its own. Your soulish realm is doing its own thing at the same time. Some people teach that a demonic spirit can just jump on you and take over your personality without your permission. If the Holy Spirit will not force Himself on you and you have the option whether to give heed to the Holy Spirit, why would you think demons would have the power to do such a thing. In light of this, I believe you have to give the permission. Demonic possession can only happen when there is some permission given, even if it is by deception or manipulation. There must be an allowance for these demons to enter in. In every instance where Jesus did cast demons out of children, He ministered through the parents. See both passages about The Syrophoenician woman *Mark 7:25-30* and paralleled in *Matthew 15:21-28*; also, see also the passages of the father whose son had a demon, see *Luke 9:37-45*. When adults had demons within them, the assumption was that they allowed the demons to gain entrance by choice.

I have heard people say, "I feel something in my spirit." When you say you feel something in your spirit are you suggesting your emotions are not a part of that? Or what about when people say my spirit is telling me to do this or the other. Are you suggesting that your mind is not involved when you are sensing the Spirit telling you something? When you say your spirit is desiring something are you then saying that does not involve your will or your desires? These three areas are intertwined and interrelated.

Spirituality involves the discipline of your mind and body. It is your mental condition that allows for spiritual growth and progress. Physical health is greatly affected by spiritual conditioning. Physical healing can take place by spiritual power exerted by the laying on of hands. This is important because when we define believing as thinking something to be true, we understand the powerful impact of using our mind to select the truth. We see the need to manage our thinking as a way of fostering great faith. The power released through faith takes place when we become skillful in knowing how to exercise our soulish faculty of thinking something to be true.

There is a solid foundation between the interrelationship of both the soul and spirit. Jesus said "...they that worship him must worship him in spirit and in truth." (John 4:24b) Truth must involve some thinking in the act of worship in one's spirit. Paul states "...renewed in the spirit of your mind; (Ephesians 4:23) Once again, suggesting a link between spirit and mind. And, what about when Paul said "...be transformed by the renewing of your mind..." *Romans 12:2.* Spiritual transformation takes place as your mind is renewed. In *Romans 7:25*, Paul said "I thank God through Jesus Christ our Lord. So then with the mind I myself serve the law of God; but with the flesh the law of sin." Paul does not say with my spirit but rather with my mind.

Another phase of this question about the interrelationship between your spirit, soul and body is what is meant by the term heart in the Bible. When the Bible says believe in your heart, or love the Lord with all your heart; what does this mean? What exactly is the heart? Once again, I always thought that the heart was separate from the mind. Although the heart is in you, I never knew how it was related to the rest of my being. It was one of those things you heard a lot about as a Christian, but you never stop to really ask what exactly is the heart anyway? But clearly, when you look closely at how the term heart is used in the scriptures, the heart has properties and abilities comparable to the mind, which may lead you to believe the heart has its own mind or its own thinking ability. For example, When Jesus said in *Matthew 5:28*, "…hath committed adultery with her already in his heart." Isn't He talking about your heart having the ability to make a choice or decide to do something? Or in *Matthew 6:21*, where He said, "For where your treasure is, there will your heart be also." Doesn't this suggest that a mental capability can be attributed to the heart? Or what about in *Matthew 9:4* when Jesus asked the Pharisees, "…Wherefore think ye evil in your hearts?" The thinking is taking place in your heart.

Once again, the area of the heart is specifically thinking in some specific way. I chose these scriptures randomly, but just about every time you see heart in both the Old and New Testaments, its referring to the heart being the center of some mental action or thinking. Consequently, it leads me to the conclusion that the heart is tied to your thinking. You cannot engage the heart without your mind being involved. I would redefine the heart as being the will of the mind. It is the place where choices are made. Decisions evolve from the mind exercises its will about something. Not only the mind, but your emotions and your desires can influence the exercising of your will by your mind. However, I do think the mind takes the lead. Your emotions and desires may impact the decision but, ultimately, the mind is the determining faculty. Believing something to be true must also be thinking something to be true and that is within the area of your mind. Emotions and desires can be unreliable because they can be contrary to the truth of God's Word. The mind has the capacity to reason what is true, and despite emotions or desires, the mind can choose to think that which is according to the Word of God.

When God revealed this to me, I asked Him when Jesus said, "And thou shalt love the Lord thy God with all thy heart, and with all thy soul, and with all thy mind, and with all thy strength: this is the first commandment." *Mark 12:30*, isn't that indicating separation? I always read that scripture, thinking these were four independent areas but His answer to me was that Jesus was describing four features of a single act of loving God. Loving God is one thing. The heart, the soul, the mind and with all your strength are all a part of the act of loving God. The heart is the will you exert from your mind; the soul is the engagement of your passion; the mind obviously is your thinking; and strength is all your effort and energy exerted. There is nothing to suggest that these areas are separate or independent of the act of loving God.

Further scripture basis for this conclusion can be found in *Matthew 15:19*; it says, "For out of the heart proceed evil thoughts, murders, adulteries, fornications, thefts, false witness, blasphemies:" The heart would have to think to have evil thoughts coming from it. It would have to conspire to commit murder. It would have to plan to commit adultery and fornication. Stealing, bearing false witness and blasphemies all would have to begin in the mind. Consequently, the heart is a part of the mind and an important feature of the will of the mind.

Whenever you see the word heart you must mean the involvement of thinking. The difference is that the heart is the will of the mind. There are many instances in the Bible where you see the word heart – and you could replace it with the word mind, and it would mean the same thing. For example, *Matthew 13:15* says, "For this people's heart (mind) is waxed gross, and their ears are dull of hearing, and their eyes they have closed; lest at any time they should see with their eyes and hear with their ears, and should understand with their heart, and should be converted, and I should heal them". Do me a favor, look at the following scriptures and replace mind in each scripture where you see heart and tell me if it means the same thing? *Matthew 5:8*, "Blessed are the pure in heart: for they shall see God." –Replace heart with mind. *Matthew 5:28* "But I say unto you, That whosoever looketh on a woman to lust after her hath committed adultery with her already in his heart." – Replace with in his mind. *Matthew 6:21*, "For where your treasure is, there will your heart be also." — Replace with your mind be also. *Matthew 11:29* "Take my yoke upon you and learn of me; for I am meek and lowly in heart: and ye shall find rest unto your souls." — Replace with lowly in mind. *Matthew 13:19* "When any one heareth the word of the kingdom, and understandeth it not, then cometh the wicked one, and catcheth away that which was sown in his heart. This is he which received seed by the way side." – Replace with sown in his mind. Especially this last example –how the Word is sown in our hearts. In order to understand something, it must involve your mind, so when you understand something in your heart isn't that involving the will of the mind? Aren't we talking about your way of thinking in terms of choosing what you will think? One definition of thinking is processing your thoughts. In the next chapter I want to talk about the processing of things in your mind.

CHAPTER 9

PROCESSING PROBLEMS

One way to describe thinking is that it is an active method of how you process things in your mind. By process I mean how you interpret or put various thoughts together to form an opinion. It is the mechanism for how we take what we are seeing and determine what our response would be to it. This may account for how two different people can see the same thing and come away with two totally different opinions of what they saw. The ten spies who saw the Promised Land saw something completely different from what Joshua and Caleb saw. The difference was in the way they processed what they saw.

There was a weakness or failing in how they were processing what God was doing. There was defect in the inner mechanism for how they handled what God did in their lives. There was a breakdown when it came to them interpreting and drawing conclusions from what God was doing in their lives. They came away from various experiences with God with an erroneous impression of what had happened. Instead of them seeing God's ways as having positive impacts and improvements for them, their disposition was of a negative posture and their cynical way of thinking made what God did, in their thinking, not good or favorable for them. Over time there was no advancement or expansion of their faith. Despite having all these miracles, signs and wonders, the needle did not move. There was no development or upswing of any kind.

Something is terribly wrong when God is blessing you and you do not see that you are enriched or better for what He is doing.

Whenever God is working in your life, you will make strides. Supposedly, you are to make progress.

This passage, *Hebrews 3:10-11* says, "Wherefore I was grieved with that generation, and said, They do alway err in their heart; and they have not known my ways." So I sware my wrath they shall not enter into my rest. *Hebrews 3:10*, is about how you can have something wrong with you that makes you incapable of being impacted for good. This is an amazing idea given the fact that God is all powerful. God can do anything and yet, you can be in a situation or position where even God cannot get through to you. All God ever desires and wants to do is to help transform you to make you better, but for some people it's like you are not open to what God is doing for you. It's as if your button is set on the off position to all God intends to do for you. As much as you may need God to bless you, there is an element where you are flat out unable to take what He is offering you.

The passage above suggests that I could be my own worst problem or my own worst enemy. I could be the very reason why I am not benefiting from being in a healthy and beautiful relationship with God. It is possible that I am shooting myself in the foot. With all that the children of Israel were up against –the cause of their downfall was themselves. It was not the hostile-inhabitable environment where there were no rivers for drinking water and there were no natural sources of food nor comfortable places where they could settle down in to sleep. It was a wilderness and it was a wilderness for a reason. It was not a coincidence that no one lived out there because it was not a place for anyone to live. No one would have chosen this as a place they would want to live. And yet God had them in the wilderness so they could learn to put their trust in Him. In the wilderness, everything had to come from God. They had nothing at all unless God provided for them. Their entire well-being depended on God's provision. They did not like this; they had a problem with this. They kept looking to find other ways to provide for themselves –other means of support. They were discontent with having to trust God. In their minds this was not good – to be totally dependent on God.

They wanted things to be different. They wanted to be more in control of their lives. Instead of the wilderness experience drawing them closer to God they became more disenchanted with God. Instead of them developing a greater appreciation for God they resented Him. Instead of learning how to trust God and getting more adept at relating to God, the opposite was the case. There was a growing tension. There was this increasing dissatisfaction and sense of frustration with being in the wilderness and having to live this way. Instead of praising God, and being grateful for all God had done for them, they blamed God and complained to Him for the situation they were in. Especially whenever they encountered misfortune or some challenge. Like when the water was bitter at Marah or when they made themselves tired of eating manna from Heaven. There was this negative attitude; this growing resentment of God for making them live like this.

The Hebrew writer wants to make it clear that the problem was not the challenges they faced. It was not the hostile and inhospitable environment they were in. The problem was not their external circumstances. The problem was them. They were their own problem.

Unbelief comes from flawed ways of thinking. When you are negative in your thinking everything you see is negative. The problem is not so much as what you see; it's really, how you see it. When you are full of negativity it clouds and impacts your perception in the sense where you cannot see anything but negativity. You even perceive negativity in God, and in all He is doing in your life.

I love this Hebrew passage because it emphasizes the need for us all to take some self-inventory and ask ourselves some hard questions. It puts the burden or weight on us, that maybe the problem is not in our circumstances but maybe the problem is the internal mechanism of how we think. Maybe it is how we process information that is the problem.

There is a different way of looking at what is going on in our lives. Could it be that I am going about all this in the wrong way and with the wrong attitude? Could the problem be how I am processing everything? Maybe it is how I am seeing things? Maybe it is the negativity in my heart that is the greater problem than the challenges I face. It is not what is against me as much as it is the way I am that makes me so miserable. Could it be that maybe it is the way I see things that make me feel so overwhelmed? Could it be that I can't trust God because I am too full of my own evil, unproductive, self-defeating ways? I want to be blessed and I need to be blessed. I have serious obstacles and barriers I need to overcome. There are looming threats to my well-being and there are unresolved issues haunting me, but the problem is not those things as much as it is an inherent defect in how I am thinking. Maybe the way I think makes it impossible for me to trust God and accept what He is doing in my life. Something is wrong when nothing God does for me is ever interpreted in a way where it is an improvement in my situation. I can't seem to get pass myself. Even when I have the good fortune of something good happening, I cannot enjoy it because inwardly I cannot allow myself to feel good about it. For whatever reason, I still tend to think of all the things that are still a problem.

A lot of us are trying to serve God but we dislike what He is doing in our lives. We disagree with His methods, His means. We don't like having to deal with the things He is using to help us and to develop us. We don't like our assignments or our work duties. We want to second guess God. We think we know better how we could get from point A to point B. We don't like having to do things God's way; we don't like to go about doing things the way He has set things up. We think we know better. We think we know a better way than the way He is going about it.

Everything God does is intended to bless you and to be a blessing to you. It may not look like a blessing. It may not feel like a blessing. It may seem uncomfortable or it may even cause some pain. But everything God does is for your good. Nothing God does ever does you any harm. The style or method of God's dealings or ways with you is that He is always doing things and moving things in a way to help you. He is doing things to facilitate your growth. He is always making you stronger and improving the overall quality of your life.

It is a trick of the devil to get you to have a bad attitude about what God is doing in your life. You are falling into a trap when you start to assume the worst about your situation. You cannot have faith for a good outcome when you are convinced that you are in a bad situation. You must believe right where you are now if you are ever going to go where God is taking you. The children of Israel could never appreciate where they were and consequently, they forfeited their opportunity to get to the Promised Land. As you can see from the Israelites, the repercussions of poor thinking can be catastrophic. Equally important is the value of good thinking, and in addition, we take note that there is no thinking more powerful than the act of remembering. In the next chapter I want to devote considerable time talking about this powerful faculty of faith.

CHAPTER 10

THE POWER OF REMEMBERING

If ways of believing are as vital as ways of thinking, it becomes important to examine ways of thinking more closely. I want to suggest to you that one of those ways of thinking, that is of extreme importance, is the development of your mindset. I am referring to when your mind remembers. In *Deuteronomy 8:2-3*, Moses encourages the children of Israel to remember the way in which the Lord led them those 40 years. The leading of the Lord had the effect of teaching them to be humble. This experience tested them. As a result, they became better people. They were able to learn about themselves, in the sense they found out some things that were contrary to the Lord in their hearts. In addition to that, they were given opportunities to see firsthand how obedience to God's Word works. They had discovered that God's commandments were the best way to go. They could see firsthand how God's commandments proved to be beneficial for them.

Remembering has to do with what you store to memory. The conclusions you draw from various experiences come from your memories of the past. It is important that you come away with things that happened concerning your past experiences with a specific impression or interpretation of what happened, which serves to affect your perspective, your attitude and your overall opinion of things. The way you store it to memory will determine whether the experience helped you or whether the experience hindered you. When your mind, for whatever reason, encounters thoughts that take you back to that experience, the question is how does the memory of this experience affect you?

Are the thoughts associated with the experience tormenting and discouraging you? When you think about the experience, is there an element of hope and joy that you get from it? Does the thought of what happened speak to you and you then now can see just how good God can be? Or is it something that scares you and makes you afraid of having to deal with that again? I believe God did things and He moved things in a specific way, with the distinct purpose that the experience will serve to empower you, equip you and make you more capable. God intentionally used methods that would produce in you the maximum, positive and potential for success. There are a few reasons why He told them, the Israelites, to remember.

First, He says remember because the most important thing related to a specific experience is how much you learned from the experience. In what ways did the experience impart key truths that have become a part of your knowledge base? Second, He tells them to remember because He wants to impact their thinking. As a result of the experience and the way in which they thought –their thinking was changed for the better. For example, concerning you; since you have changed your way of thinking and as a result of your experiences, you now focus on the right things. As a result of your experiences, you now think in terms of all the things that were possible. As a result of the experience you have included God in your thinking. Never limit yourself by only thinking in terms of what you can do or what is possible within yourself. You now think in terms of how God can do things way beyond that which is impossible for you.

Third, He wants them to remember so that the way they process new information is affected by the experiences they have already encountered. As a result of the Israelites' experiences, they processed things in such a way where they are now aware of all that is possible. All that God did for them opened them up to believe for all that He can do. Another reason why He tells them to remember is because the experiences of being led in the wilderness had stretched them and made them more adaptable so that they can handle so much more and respond to situations without feeling overwhelmed so easily.

It is important for them to remember because God allowed certain things to happen in the wilderness –to encourage them –to form certain conclusions and assumptions about what was going on. He wants you to remember because He wants certain things to be in your memory that serve to inform you and guide you in your decisions and attitude about what you are now facing. Remembering allows your memory to be a resource and source of encouragement to facilitate your now.

Your memory literally allows you to use your history and past to help you interpret the present, despite what God has done in the past for you. He says remember because He wants you to recognize the connection with what He has done and with what He is doing now. Remembering is important because God wants those things that happened to you to, hopefully, encourage you and give insight into what He is going to do now for you. He wants you to remember so that you can and will avoid the same mistakes and errors you made in the past. Remembering keeps you from assuming a new situation or an unfamiliar situation, in a negative thinking way, that God cannot bless or won't bless you now. Your memory will remind you that God has done other things to bless you and benefit you, and He can and will take care of this thing too. Remembering is the application of your memory, which allows you to draw truth and insight into how you can believe or expect God to move now. By remembering you are thinking of specific things God has done in the past. This provides the necessary basis upon which to anticipate how God will bless you now.

The opposite of remembering is forgetting. Forgetting is a real dangerous thing. Forgetting will permit or allow you to repeat the same mistakes of the past. Forgetting can and will cause you to fail in making progress. So, maybe you do not remember, or you think you did not profit from all that God has done for you. Forgetting will cause you to miss the significance and meaning of the experience. The whole point of why you went through the experience is lost because you forgot it.

Moses cites several things which should heighten our sense of gratitude. There are several significant features in which God saved us, which should make us especially thankful for what He has done for us, and we ought to always remember God for all He has already done.

First, he led you these 40 years in the wilderness; the sheer preserving power of God to keep you alive that long.

In *Deuteronomy 8:3* Moses describes how He allowed them to experience hunger just so that He could feed them with manna and teach them that man does not live by bread alone but every word that proceeds from the mouth of God.

In verse four, Moses describes how their clothes did not wear out and their feet did not swell even though they traveled for 40 years in the wilderness.

In *Deuteronomy 8:7-9*, Moses describes how God had brought them to "…a good land, a land of brooks of water, of fountains and depths that spring out of valleys and hills; A land of wheat, and barley, and vines, and fig trees, and pomegranates; a land of oil olive, and honey; A land wherein thou shalt eat bread without scarceness, thou shalt not lack any thing in it; a land whose stones are iron, and out of whose hills thou mayest dig brass." Also, verses 10-11, "When thou hast eaten and art full, then thou shalt bless the Lord thy God for the good land which he hath given thee. Beware that thou forget not the Lord thy God, in not keeping his commandments, and his judgments, and his statutes, which I command thee this day:"

God wants us to remember the extent to which we have been saved. You were saved from a lot –a whole lot. You had to be delivered from a lot –a whole lot. God does not want you to forget the extremity to which you were lost.

In *Deuteronomy 8:2* "And thou shalt remember 'all the way' which the LORD thy God led thee these forty years in the wilderness, to humble thee, and to prove thee, to know what was in thine heart, whether thou wouldest keep his commandments, or no."

It is a good thing to always remember life experiences in the context of everything you experience in life. As opposed to the individual merit of each experience, see the spiritual value of the experiences as they relate to how those things affected you for good. The sheer length of time you have been kept is astounding, as well as the sheer degree of your preservation while you were going through. The sheer difficulty with which God allowed you to overcome the experiences and challenges is enough to give you hope and faith.

Remember how good God has been in keeping you and remember how the many ways in which these experiences were orchestrated by God. God led you this way. In many ways God has shown His supernatural provisions. Primarily, He fed you in the worst of conditions. Second, He allowed you to be in a place where there was no food, and then He fed you supernaturally with food you could not take any credit for in even knowing what the food was. Instead of blessing you with what you needed within the circumstances, God blessed you with food completely outside of your circumstances. He allowed you to get to a place of extreme need so that He could cause you to be aware of just how much you needed Him to help you. You cannot fully appreciate what God has done for you until you remember the extremities with which He has blessed you.

Your spiritual faculties are aroused by your remembering. You develop a spiritual perspective by remembering all the ways God has kept you. Remembering is where you get the valid evidence for your present situation.

Remembering will release a power beyond yourself, and beyond your own resources. Remembering raises your faith so that you can believe for what God is doing. Remembering removes any strongholds or mental blockages which inhibits your capacity to do what is required in your life. Remembering allows you to see that whatever you are facing is not any greater than what you have already overcome. Remembering allows you to build on what God has done instead of starting all over again. Remembering allows you to see the big picture, and to realize that this is not any greater than the totality of everything God has already done. Remembering is the way to remain grateful and thankful. The whole lot of your thankfulness is based on remembering all God has done. Remembering allows you to find meaning and purpose instead of uncertainty and confusion.

Remembering eliminates doubts and allows you to build the case for all the reasons why you can be secure about what God will do for you. Remembering allows you to draw from passed experiences so that you can be strengthened for present situations.

Remembering enables you to be conscious of things you might not be aware of if you did not remember. Remembering allows you to learn from passed experiences so that you can be more knowledgeable about things as a result of those experiences. Learning the lessons of the past equips you for the challenges ahead. Remembering shows you how to apply your faith like you did in the past. Remembering introduces you to the spiritual realm and spiritual reality. When you remember you realize you made it solely by God's goodness. Remembering is so important because unbelief is based on an exaggeration of negative factors, which enables you to assume it is impossible to believe for what God has said in His Word. Remembering provides balance in that when you remember what God has already done, you see that He is greater than anything in your circumstances. Distrust is based on the idea that God cannot be relied upon in this situation. Remembering helps you to see just how credible God is, in that He has never let you down. Rarely can you know the value of anything you go through while you are going through it. It is only when you stop and reflect on everything can you see why certain things happened and how you benefited from them.

God wants you to be energized and full of faith. His intention for us is that we go into situations confident and expectant. God wants us to approach things with optimism and certainty, based on our experiences with Him. God intends for us to be overflowing with excitement about the opportunities we have in front of us. We cannot only win but winning is a pattern for us; we always win. God does not want us to be crippled or damaged by our past disappointments and mistakes. We are not to be overly conscious of our failures and setbacks, but rather, God intends for us to be full of faith. What God has planned for us requires us to be at our maximum output and productivity. We need to be fired up and on point. You cannot afford to be deflated, weakened or wounded by your past. If anything, your past must be the catalyst that fuels your hopes and dreams for tomorrow, in addition to preparing you with high anticipation for greater things.

Healing takes place in your mind when God's Word pulls down strongholds entrenched from bad memories related to bad experiences. God wants you to remember how He preserved you and kept you. Deliverance takes place when the memory of what happened no longer haunts and torments you, and you can function without any negative or hindering vibes coming to you from what happened. The areas where the enemy can generate the most fear are the areas where you have passed history and similar experiences. Even though you survived those trying experiences, fear for certain things was instilled in you, and the only way to overcome those fears is to remember God's role in keeping you from those dangers. You have nothing to fear because God was with you, leading you and keeping you. The breakthrough in your life is when you broke free from all the things that held you in check or held you at bay in the past. You cannot get pass your past until you remember the right way –God's way. You are not whole until your memory of certain things is corrected. If you continue to hold onto a full memory bank of negative and traumatic feelings associated with things of your past, you can never be fully whole. Any time the enemy can jerk you around and affect you in a negative way, it is a sign that God needs to correct your memory. The enemy has no more basis to bind you when your mind is corrected. Every evil emotion can be traced to some bad memory. Fears, doubts, guilt, grief, resentment, bitterness, depression –all come from bad memories.

Storing things in their rightful place for retrieval is critical. If you don't put things away in the right place you cannot find them when you need them. Computer viruses destroy files which can prevent you from functioning appropriately. Any pain or discomfort associated with your past is stored up in your memory. Healing must first target your memory, or you will never be rid of the pain. Anything you do that will address the bad memory of something will help to deliver you from the bondage associated with the things in your past. One aspect of deliverance is the reinterpretation of things that happened in the past so that the toxic, negative and binding influence of those things are removed, and they can no longer be limiting forces in your life.

Thanksgiving is the ultimate form of refilling. It is when you take something that occurred in the past and re-classify it in a different place in your mind. You characterize it in a different way; interpret it to be something better than it was perceived before. Instead of that regretful thing that happened to you, or that something you grieved about, or that something that reminds you of the worst that happened to you, you can now change how you store those incidents in your mind. Instead of it being negative, painful and deflating, it becomes something for which you are thankful; instead of conjuring up thoughts of sadness and bitterness, and instead of this reminding you of everything wrong and terrible about your past, these things are refilled as times when God blessed you the most. Those were times when God received the glory. Your life was most favored by the Lord. You look back at those times as victories, as milestones, as breakthrough times.

The existence of these bad memories and unfortunate incidents are the bases for all the strongholds and bondages in your life. These things might seem harmless, but however, they are toxic. They continue to exert influence in how you think and what you tend to think about, and they continue to influence the approach you have toward certain things. The brain has this massive storage capacity. Whenever you experience something or go through something, your brain stores it in the area of the brain called the vortex.

What sets us apart from all the other animals is this ability to store information. It allows us to adapt in a way that defines what we call, intelligence. Each time we encounter a similar situation we have the capacity to retrieve pertinent learned information and process it into making a wise decision. Conclusions, assumptions, beliefs, attitudes, aspirations, perspectives, and any other form of thought evolves from this process. Once that thought is formed it dictates your capacity to function properly and operate effectively. The nature of those thoughts has everything to do with how compatible you are to a life with God, a life in the Spirit and a life that is meaningful and satisfying. These reservoirs of thoughts are what make you what you are and determine everything that you can do.

When we talk about strongholds such as evil imaginations, high things or evil thoughts that exalts itself against the knowledge of God, *2 Corinthians 10:5,* Paul is referring to this body of information in our memory bank. It is here where everything negative and limiting comes from. It is here where you feel inadequate, incapable and inferior. This is where thoughts are generated which paralyze you and traumatize you. It is from here that you feel deflating influences; things that cause you to feel insecure and unsettled. Fear comes from the thoughts that evolve from the danger generated from this storage place in your mind. Resentment is experienced from incidents where you were offended and hurt. Eventually, resentment can develop into a root of bitterness that literally poisons you and emits or releases defiling power to others. Angry thoughts are stored here which can develop into rage and intense hatred against people. Other destructive and weakening thoughts include thoughts of grief, loss and despair which also comes from this place. And then, the most powerful one of all is guilt.

Guilt is the granddaddy of them all. The existence of guilt is the strongest category of thoughts that impact us. As a matter of fact, guilt is the root of all the other things. That is why Jesus had to come and forgive our sins so that we could get deliverance from all bondage and afflictions associated with sin. You cannot ever be free without something being done about your sins. Only when your sins are addressed can you ever get deliverance from all the other things we have just mentioned.

Those thoughts that are in your memory bank define what you are and determine your spiritual, as well as your mental condition. "For as he thinketh in his heart, so is he..." *Proverbs 23:7* Paul recognized the power of these thoughts when he says in Philippians, "Finally, brethren, whatsoever things are true, whatsoever things are honest, whatsoever things are just, whatsoever things are pure, whatsoever things are lovely, whatsoever things are of good report; if there be any virtue, and if there be any praise, think on these things. *Philippians 4:8*

We are responsible for managing the nature of these thoughts that exist in our hearts. We must not allow our minds to be dominated with the wrong kind of thoughts. We actively ensure that the information we maintain in our memory bank is helpful, beneficial, and empowering and most of all, that these thoughts are in line with God's Word. We are to challenge any foreign or conflicting thoughts that may exist in our minds. The make-up of this body of thoughts is the most important influence in your life. Either your mind is helping you, facilitating you, enhancing you or it is having the opposite effect, that is limiting you, afflicting you, weighing you down and even poisoning you.

What makes the Word of God so important is that it is a medium of change of healing and repair. It has the capacity to change this negative body of thoughts into positive energy and a force for good. Literally, the Word of God has the power to transform these thoughts from debilitating, deflating and restrictive — to liberating, empowering and restorative thoughts. The Word of God can make you resilient, strong and stable. The Word of God can literally cleanse away the foreign matter or inappropriate ingredients that cause evil influences. It can neutralize the work of thoughts that are entrenched in our minds — holding up free movement of thoughts that we need to have. It is those thoughts that are planted in places that block and obstruct certain things from coming forth or coming to pass. These things are strategically located in key places to prevent key activities and important processes for handling information. For example, these thoughts can stand in the way of allowing you to have joy or enjoy certain kinds of things. These thoughts can keep you from experiencing peace. These things generate phobias and uncontrollable fears of certain things. They can block the passage of thoughts associated with victory, security and optimism. Whenever you need to be confident these entrenched thoughts block those thoughts and create uncertainty and chaos.

Change cannot happen for the good if you continue the negative body of thoughts; these negative body of thoughts are made up of the wrong kinds of things. Every evil habit, every bad attitude and every evil tendency from addictions to self-destructive behaviors originate from this negative body of thoughts. Change in this pool of thoughts will bring about change in how you think. Change in how you think is the most important change salvation can bring to pass in your life. The Holy Spirit is exposing those thoughts so that the Word of God can take precedence over them. That is why Paul says in *Romans 12:2* "And be not conformed to this world: but be ye transformed by the renewing of your mind..." In *Ephesians 4:23*, he says "And be renewed in the spirit of your mind;"

Your personal power is determined by the make-up of this pool of key thoughts. Your ability to react to situations is dictated to by this pool of thoughts. Your capacity to relate to God and experience intimacy in relationship to God is determined by this pool of thoughts. Your ability to exercise faith is determined by the existence of evil, ungodly and negative thoughts. I believe that is what defines unbelief, or disbelief. Unbelief is defined as the existence of conflicting information that blocks your ability to accept the spiritual reality of God's Word.

The power of these evil thoughts is determined by the length of time they have been in your heart. These evil thoughts grow and become more and more entrenched over time, and they increase in power as they're allowed to go unchallenged. The placement of these thoughts or position in your life is important in determining just how strong these thoughts are in your life. When these thoughts are in critical areas, they can have a devastating effect on you. For example, if they are in areas like self-esteem and self-worth, they literally could wreak havoc. When they are in places like the ability to learn or the capacity to relate to others, they can have a major impact. If they are in the area of how you perceive God or what you perceive God to be, they can seriously affect your capacity to relate to God.

Another factor that can determine the intensity of these thoughts is the source of them. If these thoughts came from people who were authoritative figures or people that you were vulnerable to because you counted them credible, then their words could literally curse you. Last but certainly not least, if these thoughts are allowed to attach themselves to other evil thoughts and become a combination of evil thoughts that tend to make them more powerful, then demonic spirits can travel in groups and they will want to join in with other evil spirits whenever they find a comfortable place.

This is a good place to talk about how the Blood of Jesus cleanses our minds. Because of the finished work of Jesus Christ on the cross, our sins were forgiven, and a process was set up to address living free from the effects of sin. The worst effects of sin are what happens to your thinking. Your mind is the main area of which the Blood of Jesus corrects and sets on the right path. Especially the memory, which must be reconditioned and repaired so that your mind functions properly and effectively.

The stress on you can be related to prior painful and traumatic experiences that have stored bad memories and thoughts, associated with something from your past. There are some painful and traumatic experiences that we may encounter in life which can cause us the most stress, which can remind us of other experiences. Suppressed sadness can manifest itself whenever something related to the cause of the depression is encountered. Difficulty in relating to some people can be traced to some bad interaction or breakdown in the past that impacts your capacity to function effectively with people in the present. The emotional baggage of the past can limit your ability to freely relate to people now. Nervousness and anxiety can be generated from the memory of some negative experiences which can cause you to overreact and become unsteady in the performance of various situations. A lack of confidence can be the result of some stored up negative experiences that impacts your capacity to approach things with optimism and assurance. Frustration or stored up frustration can cause your reaction to not only be fed by what is happening currently, but also the cumulative impact of all the past experiences which join with what is going on in the present, to trigger a more intense reaction. Many times, pain and fatigue can be built up over time, which may cause a breakdown that is not caused by the current response to a specific situation. All bondages come from evil thoughts or mental blockages implanted in our memory bank. This can assist in influencing us in all areas related to specific experiences, impressions and life experiences learned from the past.

The specific tasks or things you cannot do can be traced to the presence of something evil and binding in your memory bank. The inability to have faith in specific areas is due to the presence of some foreign lie existing inside your mind. I am a firm believer that the Blood of Jesus cleanses the mind. As the blood flows through your memory bank, the Blood of Jesus cleanses your mind from any infiltration and damage that may be the result of your sin. Divine healing is the result of the Blood of Jesus flowing to that area, carrying the Word you received in your mind and in your heart. When you receive and believe the truth of God's Word the composition of your blood receives an injection which in turn flows to the area in need of healing. As the Blood releases the power from the revealed Word, there is a chemical reaction in which the Word heals that area. In the natural, it is as you breathe in the oxygen that comes through your lungs, the blood carries that oxygen to the heart where it is pumped throughout the rest of your body. As it reaches various parts of your body, the blood releases the oxygen as fuel for your body to function. In the same way, as you ingest the Spirit, which in Hebrew and Greek means breath or wind, the Blood empowering your entire being carries the Spirit, filling you up with spiritual life and literally, quickening your mortal body. *Romans 8:6* says, "For to be carnally minded is death but to be spiritually minded is life and peace." Whenever you get a heightened level of reaction to something, your body releases a hormone called adrenaline. This hormone equips and prepares the body to respond to some danger or threat. It supplies the body with increased levels of oxygen and raises the heart rate to pump so that you can function at a level where you can meet the challenge at hand. The problem is, after the threat has subsided, there is no more need to be at this heightened state of alert, and there are remnants of these hormones still present in your blood stream. Elevated quantities of hormones have an eroding toxic effect on your body, impacting your immune system which fights the development of sicknesses and diseases. Study has shown that scientists have linked stress levels with causing damage to a human being's immune system. The value of the Blood of Jesus is when it is activated by the Word of God; the Blood of Jesus cleanses the blood supply and neutralizes these harmful toxins. In chemistry, certain chemicals or elements can neutralize other elements, making them no longer dangerous or toxic. The infusion of certain chemicals can change the properties of a specific element to even make that element perform some necessary function. In the same way the Blood of Jesus serves to neutralize any toxic or poisonous thoughts or impressions lodged in your memory bank, ending the danger or threat caused by its existence. In the medical arena one of the specific measures taken is to ensure that there is a clean environment. Where there is bacteria or dirt of any kind of uncleanness, there is opportunity for worsening medical conditions caused by infections, viruses and the compromise of our immune system. No doctor treats you with medical instruments that are not clean and sterilized. In the same way, no ministry can be effective if there is not an emphasis on providing a clean environment. Especially your blood supply, because anytime something foreign is introduced into your blood supply, there is an immediate reaction to your body. Your blood carries this foreign intrusion to the rest of your body, spreading damages as it goes. Sometimes the blood supply can be so tainted that they will have to give you a blood transfusion to introduce healthy blood back into your system. There are some church environments where many people go to seek spiritual help and, unfortunately, some of these environments eventually end up being places where they are introduced to damaged and uncleanness, which then makes the environment worst as a result of having been exposed to contamination and uncleanness. When people have dirty hearts and unclean spirits, they literally transfer their uncleanness to those to whom they minister. Spirits like fear and anger can be contagious and as a result of someone having these spirits, they can communicate these spirits to people who receive their words or ministry.

Healing in the mind releases power that is introduced into the blood stream which then flows through your body, giving you the power to do the things you need to do. When something is corrected in your mind, it has a direct effect on everything else about you, your attitude, your health, your perspective and your overall sense of well-being. Jesus always ministered to a person's mind in order to minister healing and deliverance. The root cause of a person's ailment was more so in the mind than anything else. When the Word was received in the person's mind, then the outward symptom was lifted, and the person could be freed from the binding condition. For example, Jesus announced or gave the Word to people and the Word went straight to what they were thinking in their minds. "...Woman, thou art loosed from thine infirmity." Or what about "...Thy sins be forgiven thee..." Or in some cases Jesus told people to do things which unlocked the overriding assumptions that caused them to be bound by some condition. For example, "...Rise, take up thy bed, and walk", or when Jesus said "...See thou tell no man; but go thy way, shew thyself to the priest..." And Jesus also said "...Stretch forth thine hand. And he stretched it forth; and it was restored whole, like as the other."

The inability to function spiritually or according to the Word is due to some evil assumptions or beliefs you continue to have present in your memory bank. Anytime the Word is applied to that something, you are freed by the power of God that has flowed from your mind through your blood supply. For example, you can only believe through your spirit. But there are things you cannot believe because there is some conflicting assumption that obstructs your spirit from grasping the spiritual reality of God's Word. Certain evil attitudes can exist and make you unable to believe certain related things like guilt, fear, and bitterness. You can only worship, that is true worship, through your spirit. When you believe the wrong things, you cannot offer real worship. Jesus told the woman at the well "...when the true worshippers shall worship the Father in spirit and in truth..." *John 4:23*. The things you cannot do can be traced to the presence of something evil and binding in your memory bank. The inability to have faith in various areas is due to the presence of some foreign false lies existing inside you.

In my next forthcoming book, I will share some insights from the Book of James, the brother of Jesus. The application of appropriate thinking is what stands out to me in James' Epistle. James presents faith in a context that makes it about practical wisdom.

God Bless.